C0-AUN-938

Becoming
An
Unwed
Mother

Montante Family Library
D'Youville College

Becoming
An
Unwed
Mother

A
Sociological
Account

Prudence
Mors
Rains

AldineTransaction
A Division of Transaction Publishers
New Brunswick (U.S.A.) and London (U.K.)

First paperback printing 2007
Copyright © by Prudence Mors Rains.

All rights reserved under International and Pan-American Copyright Conventions. No part of this book may be reproduced or transmitted in any form or by any means, electronic or mechanical, including photocopy, recording, or any information storage and retrieval system, without prior permission in writing from the publisher. All inquiries should be addressed to AldineTransaction, A Division of Transaction Publishers, Rutgers—The State University, 35 Berrue Circle, Piscataway, New Jersey 08854-8042. www.transactionpub.com

This book is printed on acid-free paper that meets the American National Standard for Permanence of Paper for Printed Library Materials.

Library of Congress Catalog Number: 2007060657
ISBN: 978-0-202-30955-2
Printed in the United States of America

Library of Congress Cataloging-in-Publication Data

Rains, Prudence.
  Becoming an unwed mother : a sociological account / Prudence Mors
  Rains.
     p. cm.
  Originally published: Chicago : Aldine-Atherton, 1971.
  ISBN 978-0-202-30955-2 (alk. paper)
   1. Unmarried mothers—United States.   2. Illegitimate children—United
  States.   I. Title.

HV700.5.R17   2007
306.874'320973—dc22   2007060657

7V 700.5
.R17
2007

JUN 15 2007

TO JACK AND ELLIOTT

Acknowledgments

This book was originally written as a dissertation in sociology at Northwestern University. Contrary to many rightly made criticisms of graduate education, I did not find my own graduate education to be rigid, parochial, or impersonal. For this, I feel a special debt to the Sociology Department at Northwestern University, particularly to the members of my doctoral committee: John Kitsuse, whose attention and interest can only be described as lavish; Howard Becker, whose benign persistence has served as an example and motive to me, as to many others; and Paul Bohannon, of the Anthropology Department, who provided me with practical help as well as his interest.

During the year I spent at Brandeis University, Irving Zola made lengthy and helpful comments about my field notes from the Project, and Stephen Miller helped me to acquire the National Science Foundation grant that supported the study I made of Hawthorne House.

Additionally, I feel an intellectual debt to the writings of Erving Goffman, David Matza, Lee Rainwater, and Harold Garfinkel; but they are in no way responsible for what I have made of their work in this book.

I owe a very special debt to the staffs and girls at the institutions that I have called the Project, Hawthorne House, and Kelman Place. Maternity homes are understandably cautious about jeopardizing their clients' wishes for secrecy and their right to go through a difficult experience with a minimum amount of intrusion. My analysis has a great deal to say—some of which is critical—about the orientations of professional social workers toward unwed mothers. Yet it is to the open-mindedness and research orientations of professional social workers that I owe my research and this book.

I owe a very great deal to the trust and grace with which the pregnant girls who came to these places accepted my presence among them. From the Project, I am particularly indebted to the girl I have called Rowena for her candor and natural sociological eye. From Hawthorne House, I am grateful to Dr. Hildreth and the eleven girls in his therapy group for their permission to observe and participate in their sessions.

Finally, I wish to thank the five girls who conducted the interviews regarding contraceptive use among college girls, reported in the first chapter. Because I have not identified the college, I cannot identify them, but I wish to acknowledge the good work they did.

Contents

Introduction

Becoming an unwed mother is the outcome of a particular sequence of events that begins with forays into intimacy and sexuality, results in pregnancy, and terminates in the birth of an illegitimate child. Many girls do not have sexual relations before marriage. Many who do, do not get pregnant. And most girls who get pregnant while unmarried do not end up as unwed mothers.[1] Girls who become unwed mothers, in this sense, share a common career that consists of the steps by which they came to be unwed mothers rather than brides, the clients of abortionists, contraceptively prepared lovers, or virtuous young ladies.

1. Exact estimations of premarital sexual intercourse, premarital conception, and outcome are complicated by the methodological difficulties of acquiring representative samples, and by the relation of these behaviors to such factors as age at marriage, social class, and race. The evidence of Alfred C. Kinsey et al., in *Sexual Behavior in the Human Female* (New York: Simon & Schuster, 1953) suggests that nearly half of married women had premarital sexual intercourse. Paul H. Gebhard et al., *Pregnancy, Birth and Abortion* (New York: John Wiley, 1958) suggest that nearly one-fifth of these conceived premaritally. About six per cent of these premaritally conceived pregnancies ended in the birth of an illegitimate child. These figures however exclude Negro women and lower-class white women.

The most significant aspects of this career are moral ones,[2] for sexuality, pregnancy, and motherhood are matters closely linked to conceptions of feminine respectability and intimately connected to women's conceptions of themselves. Becoming an unwed mother is not simply a private and practical trouble; it is the kind of trouble that forces public accounting, raises retrospective questions, and, above all, calls into question the kind of person the unwed mother was and is.

The moral career of an unwed mother is, in this sense, like the moral careers of other persons whose acts are treated as deviant, and whose selves become publicly implicated. Important, if not central, to the moral career of such a person are the social agencies with which he may come into contact as a result of his situation. Social agencies and institutions, whether geared to rehabilitation, incarceration, help, or punishment, provide and enforce interpretations of the person's current situation, of the past that led to it, and of the possibilities that lie ahead. Agencies may do this explicitly, presenting their interpretations as professional understandings based on research and experience. Or, as Erving Goffman (1961) has so extensively observed, agencies may do this less explicitly through routines for handling clients which contain an implicit statement about the sort of person being dealt with.

This is a study of the moral career of the unwed mother, particularly as this career is shaped by social agencies. The study draws on the experiences of two quite different groups

2. I have borrowed the conception of "moral career" from Erving Goffman's analysis of the situation of mental patients, "The Moral Career of the Mental Patient," *Asylums* (Chicago: Aldine, 1961), pp. 125–169. In that essay, *career* is used to refer to the "changes over time as are basic and common to the members of a social category"; the moral aspects of career are, then, "the regular sequence of changes that career entails in the person's self and in his framework of imagery for judging himself and others" (pp. 127–128).

of girls during the time they spent in two quite different institutions for unwed mothers. It deals with the experiences of girls during pregnancy—with consequences rather than cause. For while unwed mothers may justify attention as a social problem requiring explanation, they justify more attention as the object of responses which return them to normality. Analyses of other deviant careers have provided insights into the processes of rejection, stigmatization, and exclusion; the moral career of the unwed mother provides an alternate view into the processes of normalization and moral reinstatement.

Most of what has been written about unwed mothers has been concerned explicitly with cause and implicitly with pathology.[3] The prime question has been what distinguishes girls who become unwed mothers from those who do not, and the answers have been sought in the long-term features of girls' backgrounds and personalities. Unwed mothers are usually compared, implicitly or explicitly, with girls who have not become pregnant.[4] The major difficulty with these causal studies arises from the equation of two related but different matters—unwed mothers and illegitimate preg-

3. This literature has been reviewed and summarized in Charles E. Bowerman et al., *Unwed Motherhood: Personal and Social Consequences* (Chapel Hill: University of North Carolina Institute for Research in Social Science, 1963–1966), in Clark E. Vincent, *Unmarried Mothers* (New York: Free Press, 1961), and in an unpublished manuscript of Wyatt Jones, "Review of the Literature Relating to Unmarried Mothers" (1967).

There have recently begun to be exceptions to the causal approach to unwed motherhood—notably the studies of Bowerman et al. (1963–1966), Furstenberg et al. (1969), and Teele et al. (1966). It is worth noting that these studies include lower-class Negro girls and women and are marked by a concern for describing their situation following pregnancy.

4. Clark Vincent's (1961) study has made this comparison most explicitly and most systematically and is, in this sense and to date, the only study of unwed mothers in which the methodology is fully suitable to a theoretical concern with cause.

nancy. Most girls who become pregnant while unmarried do not become unwed mothers, but instead become wives or the clients of abortionists (Gebhard et al., 1958). The causes of illegitimate pregnancy cannot, therefore, be understood from the study of unwed mothers. There is even some ambiguity as to what the social problem is, and in what sense illegitimate pregnancy is in itself a social problem.[5]

Even ignoring this sort of confusion, there is virtually no evidence that unwed mothers share any special characteristics which distinguish them from girls who have not become pregnant (Vincent, 1961; Jones, 1967).

I have, therefore, not made the assumption that critical psychological or motivational differences distinguish unwed mothers from other girls. I have preferred instead to look for the concerns which link the early stages of normal sexual careers with the stages which produce unwed mothers. And I have preferred to understand the special concerns and moral experiences of unwed mothers in relation to the more usual concerns of unmarried girls in coming to terms with sexuality and respectability.

The first chapter is, in a sense, a defense and fuller statement of that preference, offering a way of understanding illegitimate pregnancy as the incidental product of the way sexual activity is *normally* organized among unmarried girls in this society. The discussion is speculative, drawing primarily on the literature dealing with premarital sexual relations and, to a lesser extent, on a small pilot study of contraceptive use among sexually experienced college girls. The first chapter can be read in three ways: as a description of the moral aspects of normal sexual careers, as an alternate

5. Illegitimate pregnancy, after all, produces many more wives than unwed mothers, except among Negroes. And for Negroes, it is perhaps more accurate to say that the social problem has less to do with unwed motherhood per se than with social conditions that make marriage an undesirable solution and abortion an unobtainable one.

hypothesis about the sources of illegitimate pregnancy, and finally, as a description of what is, for those girls who become pregnant and go on to have an illegitimate child, the first phase in their moral careers as unwed mothers.

The remaining chapters deal directly with the experiences of girls who became unwed mothers in the institutions I have identified as the Project, a day school for young Negro girls, and Hawthorne House, a psychiatrically oriented residential maternity home.

The second chapter draws on the girls' recollections of their experiences before arriving at either place, to describe their concerns upon finding themselves pregnant and to comment more generally on the process of arriving at some solution to the problem of illegitimate pregnancy. The second half of the chapter departs from the girls' experiences to describe the traditional orientations and practices of maternity homes, exemplified by Kelman Place, a residential maternity home at which I spent some time. Kelman Place is used to point out the departures from traditional orientations being made by institutions like the Project and Hawthorne House and also to suggest that, in spite of these departures, institutions for unwed mothers nevertheless share some structural features which sponsor an initial experience of moral reprieve for their clients. The second chapter therefore describes the materials—experiences of the girls in coming to reveal their situation to others and the nature of the institutions to which they eventually came—which transform moral jeopardy into an initial sense of moral reprieve. For the pregnant girl, it is a transformation from a feared version of herself as a sexually promiscuous girl to a version of herself as an unwed mother, a girl who made a mistake.

For the girl who enters Hawthorne House, this view of herself is temporary, for she encounters an explicit and systematically expressed psychiatric view of herself and her situation. The third chapter describes the psychiatric and moral orientations of the Hawthorne House staff toward their clients, orientations which are organized around a version of the past, on the one hand, and around becoming a mother, on the other hand. The fourth chapter describes what girls make of the House orientations, the moral career of the girl who becomes an unwed mother at Hawthorne House.

The fifth and sixth chapters deal with the situation during pregnancy of a quite different group of girls—young Negro girls who planned to keep their babies and who commuted daily to the Project school from home. The fifth chapter describes the staff orientations toward the girls and their situation, orientations which were expressed in regular group counseling sessions and which, for a variety of reasons, were resisted by the Project girls. The sixth chapter describes the moral career of the Negro unwed mother, a career which, for the Project girls, was shaped less by the Project than by a set of accommodations learned from public response to their situation.

The final chapter steps back from the moral experiences of unwed mothers to comment critically on the nature and sources of illegitimacy as a social problem and to suggest the services which might most usefully be addressed to the problems generated by illegitimate pregnancy and illegitimacy.

I

The Situation of Moral Jeopardy

1

Sexual Careers

It is most favorable for the sexual initiation if, without violence or surprise and without set procedure or calculated delay, the young girl slowly learns to overcome her modesty, to know her partner, and to enjoy his love-making . . . . The initiation is facilitated as it loses its tabooed aspect, as the girl feels more free with respect to her partner. . . .

SIMONE DE BEAUVOIR
The Second Sex (1952 : 365–366)

Most of what has been written about unwed mothers has been concerned explicitly with cause, and implicitly with pathology—with the special features which distinguish unwed mothers from other girls. I have signaled my general intention to deal in this study with the consequences rather than the causes of illegitimate pregnancy. This chapter stands as a partial exception to that intention, however, for it presents a way of understanding the sources of illegitimate pregnancy which does not invoke notions of pathology. As an alternate way of dealing with the question of cause, the chapter is speculative; as a way of presenting the moral aspects of normal sexual careers, and as a way of locating the special concerns of girls who become pregnant, it is descriptive.

9

Because I have drawn on a variety of studies, it will be useful to preview the major points.

First, most girls in the course of their lives prior to marriage alter their moral standards and sexual behavior, generally becoming more permissive. This process can be viewed as an anticipation of marriage, as a coming to some terms with intimacy and sexuality.

Second, the central moral experience of premarital sexual careers is that of ambivalence and guilt which is imposed not so much by external norms, but by the experience of acting in ways which girls themselves have only recently regarded, and perhaps still regard, as unacceptable. Premarital sexual careers are, in this sense, experienced as deviant careers.

Third, the central problems of premarital sexual careers are the closely interwoven problems of self-respect and reputation. Girls must reconcile their behavior with a view of themselves as essentially respectable and, in order to do this, must maintain their reputation in the eyes of others as essentially nonpromiscuous.

Fourth, the conventions and common practices of dating and of premarital sexual activity can be viewed as social structures which allow girls to maintain a view of themselves as reasonably conventional, reasonably virtuous, and morally respectable persons while nevertheless participating in activity which exceeds their current moral standard. These conventions, by neutralizing internal disapproval, allow such participation. One of these conventions, having to do with contraceptive use, is relevant to the issue of illegitimate pregnancy.

The fifth point, therefore, is that illegitimate pregnancy, particularly among middle-class girls, can be understood as a product of reputational concerns which all girls share and not the product of any *particular* deviant motivations among those who become pregnant.

My intent in the following elaboration of these points is to provide a description of what is, for those girls who become pregnant and go on to have an illegitimate child, the first phase of their moral careers as unwed mothers.

PREMARITAL SEXUAL CAREERS

Moral discussion of premarital sexual experience typically polarizes around the issue of sexual intercourse, treating this issue as the prime moral question facing unmarried girls and as the source of most of the moral uncertainty girls experience in the course of their premarital sexual careers. Moral recommendations, whether made by liberal or conservative critics of the current sexual scene, are addressed to this particular source of uncertainty. Too exclusive a focus on sexual intercourse, however, obscures the extent to which all girls share similar moral experiences in coming to terms with intimacy and sexuality regardless of the modesty or permissiveness of their moral standards or sexual behavior.

On the one hand, champions of premarital sexual freedom, believing that the sexual revolution has occurred or ought to, tend to overlook the difficulties and ambivalence currently experienced by girls in arriving at a liberated view of their own sexuality. For while some girls in this society may grow up in circumstances which favor an open avowal of sexual freedom, most do not.

Current adult opinion opposes premarital sexual intercourse; even student opinion, which is more permissive, does not favor it. Ira Reiss, who has undertaken the most recent national sample survey on the subject, reports 86 per cent of the adults surveyed held a standard for young people which excludes intercourse even for engaged couples. For a sample of high school and college students he reports 68 per cent of the females and 55 per cent of the males as holding a similarly restricted standard. (Reiss, 1967 : 26–27)

A girl who does participate in full sexual relations before she marries does so surrounded by what is, at best, unsupportive opinion which must be handled if she is to feel at ease with her behavior. While many girls do manage to come to an open and unconflicted acceptance of premarital sexual intercourse, most are not likely to have begun their dating careers with this view and will have experienced uncertainty in reaching this view.

Even an open and genuine acceptance of premarital sexual intercourse does not eliminate all sources of moral conflict in premarital sexual relations; such a position simply opens a new set of moral issues—for example, the exclusiveness of one's sexual relationships.

On the other hand, maintenance of high moral standards does not eliminate moral conflict or bypass problems of respectability, although this is implied in the recommendations of spokesmen for a more conventional morality. Even mild forms of sexual activity raise problems of respectability and reputation; the risk of seeming loose, fast, promiscuous is present even in such innocuous matters as appropriate dress and demeanor, and is made particularly salient by the ambiguity of norms for activities falling short of sexual intercourse. A girl who never accepts sexual intercourse for herself must nevertheless concern herself not simply with the moral matter of *being* respectable, but with the practical matter of *seeming* respectable[1]—fitting even quite acceptable behavior to a sense of right occasion and potential reputational consequence.

1. Erving Goffman (1959 : 251) has described this dilemma more generally and extensively: "In their capacity as performers, individuals will be concerned with maintaining the impression that they are living up to the many standards by which they and their products are judged. Because these standards are so numerous and so pervasive, the individuals who are performers dwell more than we might think in a moral world. But, *qua* performers, individuals are concerned not with the moral issue of realizing these standards but with the amoral issue of engineering a convincing impression that these standards are being realized . . . the very obligation and profitability of appearing always in a steady moral light, of being a socialized character, forces one to be the sort of person who is practiced in the ways of the stage."

Partisans of a strict moral standard also tend to overlook the extent to which even the most modest girl will experience some necessity to alter the moral standards of her early youth and, in making this transition, will experience some uncertainty about what specifically constitutes a high moral standard.

Ira Reiss observes that most (85 per cent) of the girls in his sample began their sexual careers with a standard which allowed kissing only, but that by the time they were twenty-one, nine out of ten of these girls accepted either petting (65 per cent) or sexual intercourse (25 per cent). Most girls in his sample experienced at least two shifts toward a more permissive standard during their premarital sexual careers. Reiss observes further that 87 per cent of the girls in his sample had at one time felt guilty about sexual behavior they later came to accept (Reiss, 1967 : 106–21).

While girls may experience such specific issues as sexual intercourse as moral problems, the previous evidence suggests that, in a larger and more structural sense, all girls share one moral experience regardless of the modesty or permissiveness of their standards and behavior.

The central figure of premarital sexual careers is the experience of coming to view as acceptable what was previously viewed as unacceptable, of acting in ways which are not yet acceptable to oneself but which will come to be acceptable. Premarital sexual careers, involving changes of this kind, are a kind of deviant career—not so much in the sense that cultural standards are violated, but in the sense that the participants find themselves violating their own standards and therefore put themselves in the position of having to agree with potential criticism. That is, most girls, regardless of the standard they hold upon marriage, will have experienced some guilt, some sense of moral vulnerability by virtue of acting in ways which they themselves have only recently regarded, or perhaps still regard, as unacceptable. At a number of points in their premarital sexual careers, most girls are likely to feel susceptible to criticism should their behavior be singled out for question or comment. It is in this sense that the link between reputation and self-respect is particularly close in periods of transition between standards, for it is at these times that a girl will feel least certain of the rightness of her behavior and be most vulnerable to others' definitions of the kind of person she is.

Because of the privacy and circumspection which surrounds premarital sexual exploration, relatively few girls experience the kind of direct confrontation with full public knowledge and comment on their behavior that is experienced, for example, by girls who become pregnant. The genuine shock which these girls report upon finding themselves pregnant suggests in fact that many girls not only manage to avoid a direct confrontation with the opinions of others but also manage to evade a confrontation with their own ambivalence. That is, most girls are able to sustain a view of themselves as essentially respectable while nevertheless acting in ways which they themselves regard as nonideal and morally dubious.

Researchers into other areas of deviant activity, activity which strikes us as a good deal more deviant than premarital sexual exploration, have pointed to the ways in which persons are able to evade a deviant self-conception. Albert Reiss (1961), for example, discusses the ways in which young male homosexual prostitutes structure their homosexual activity so as to define themselves as casual entrepreneurs rather than as homosexuals or prostitutes. The definition of self as essentially conventional structures unconventional activity.

David Matza and Gresham Sykes (Sykes and Matza, 1957; Matza, 1964), in their reflections on juvenile delinquency, suggest that an important factor in facilitating this sort of uncommitted deviance is in fact the availability of some set of justifications or qualifications which serve to neutralize internal disapproval in advance of the act. They provide a lengthy analysis of the ways in which delinquents justify, excuse, mitigate their acts, drawing their justifications from the very legal code they violate. Matza and Sykes are careful to stress that this legalistic talk is not mere rationalization after the fact; it is rather a way of neutralizing internal disapproval before the fact, and therefore a kind of limit on possible acts. Techniques of neutralization both allow and structure participation in unconventional activity by persons who regard themselves as conventional.

Applying this framework to premarital sexual careers, the conventions of dating and of premarital sexual exploration can be viewed as social structures which allow girls to sustain a view of themselves as reasonably conventional and essentially virtuous. These conventions, shaped to the requirements of reputation-maintenance, serve to neutralize the internal disapproval a girl may feel in anticipation of nonideal conduct, thereby supporting one of several possible definitions of the girl and her situation.

The conventions used here as examples include the condition of love, the dating pattern of serial monogamy, the arrangement of sexual participation in qualitative stages over time, the maintenance of technical virginity, and the structured use or nonuse of contraceptive methods. Not all girls will pattern their sexual participation in these ways; obviously some of these conventions characterize some stages of sexual participation and not others. Those girls who do pattern their sexual participation in these ways, however, will be more likely to maintain their reputations as essentially nonpromiscuous in their own and others' eyes. For these conventions preserve the reluctant stance toward sexual expression expected of unmarried girls in this culture.

The Condition of Love

The major technique of neutralization is love, and its conventional source is marriage. That is, love is the condition which justifies and allows participation in what has pre- viously been viewed as unacceptable sexual activity— whether kissing or sexual intercourse. The notion that love legitimates sexual expression derives from the view that sex- ual relations are the major way in which husbands and wives express their love for each other.

There is a great deal of evidence that for girls there is a strong relationship between being in love and shifts toward more permissive behavior and more permissive standards. Ehrmann (1960 : 337) feels this to be the most significant finding of his study of premarital dating behavior. Ira Reiss observes, for his sample, that only 40 per cent of the girls whose standard included only kissing had been in love, while 60 per cent of those who accepted petting and 78 per cent of those who accepted intercourse had been in love (Reiss, 1967 : 114).

It is possible to view this link between love and sexual expression as natural, at least natural to women. However, it is also useful to see that the requirement of love serves reputational purposes. That is, there are a number of ways in which the requirement of love as a justification for sex- ual expression protects girls from imputations regarding character.

First, a girl's reputation probably depends not so much on her own standard as it does on the relationship between her standard and the standard expected of her by the boys she dates. It is not unlikely that she will date boys who hold a more restrictive standard for her than she may hold for her- self. It is also likely that she will not necessarily and initially be able to infer a boy's standard from his behavior. Condi- tioning sexual expression on love has the important conse- quence of giving a girl time to assess the boy and his stan- dards for judging her.

Love is a mutual relationship involving mutual concern. The requirement of love for any sexual activity therefore has the second consequence of allowing the girl to have more control, in a more pleasant manner, over how sexual activity advances than she might otherwise have. The accusation of sexual teasing is more likely to be applied to a girl who will participate in sexual activity up to a point with a casual acquaintance than to a girl who acts the same way with a boy she loves and who loves her.

Third, the requirement of a love relationship tends to insure secrecy about the specific nature and extent of sexual activity, mirroring the kind of privacy which bounds marriage. As the relationship deepens and sexual intimacy progresses sufficiently to be assumed by others, this sort of discretion becomes less necessary for the girl is protected from being viewed as a general sexual object by the exclusiveness of her relationship with her boyfriend. Nevertheless, even in marriage, sexuality's expected province, too specific talk about private sexual matters with others is viewed as a kind of disloyalty.

Because love is understood to be an extenuating condition for sexual activity in the eyes of others, it is politic for a girl to love those with whom she participates in sexual activity and to require love, or the vocabulary of love, of them. Ira Reiss observes, somewhat cynically, that "a female may act as though she believes a man who says 'I love you' in order to make him think she would not have indulged unless she thought he loved her" (Reiss, 1960 : 162). It is doubtful that many girls feel the kind of self-assurance to be so coolly and practically concerned with reputation as Reiss suggests. The requirement of love for sexual activity is as much an internal rhetoric as it is an external rhetoric, solving problems of moral ambivalence and issues of self-respect as well as more practical reputational problems.

Patterns of Premarital Sexual Activity

Participation in premarital sexual activity, justified generally in terms of love, is itself patterned in ways which have relevance for the issues of reputation and self-respect.

Exclusive dating, which over several relationships forms a pattern of serial monogamy, can be looked at as the structural correlate of the requirement of love, as love is generally understood. That is, currently sanctioned notions of love hold it to be an exclusive emotion justifying sexual involvement with one person only. Any girl who borrows love as the conventional justification for sexual involvement must also borrow the view that love is exclusive.

However, serial monogamy can only be an approximate pattern of dating careers that include more than one or two serious relationships and periods of uncertainty as to which boy a girl really loves. The classic example is the college girl whose allegiance wavers between the boy from home and the boy at school. Rather than view the pattern of serial monogamy as a description of the bulk of most girls' dating careers, it is perhaps more accurate to look at exclusive dating as a standard which is approximated as girls become involved in greater sexual intimacy, and as they experience the tensions in steady but not exclusive dating. Most girls date steadily, although not necessarily exclusively, going out with several boys a number of times rather than with many boys a few times (Schofield, 1965 : 74–78). Steady dating sponsors the growth of fondness, love, and sexual intimacy—quite possibly with more than one boy. As sexual involvement increases, however, exclusive dating is the only pattern which lends credence to the assertion of love, justifying intimacy and supporting the definition of a girl's situation as essentially respectable.

The second pattern of premarital sexual activity are the stages of sexual activity—stages of permissiveness which are experienced as qualitatively different. For example, petting under clothes is not simply experienced as a more permissive continuation of petting over clothes but as a qualitatively more permissive activity. The matter of standards or "drawing the line" is a matter of settling upon lines which are commonly understood to define the stages of permissiveness.

Even a firm moral standard, however, merely defines a presumably ultimate limit. How that limit is reached in the context of a relationship with one boy is also a moral matter with consequences for self-respect and reputation. Formal studies of premarital sexual behavior have been concerned largely with how far a girl has gone and how often rather than with how she got there in the context of a relationship. The matter of timing, as a practical and moral concern, has been restricted to the advice columns of magazines geared to teen-age girls. Note the quantities of discussion in such magazines devoted to the seemliness of kissing a boy on the first, second, or third date. While these magazines maintain a discreet silence on the more intricate question of what is appropriate and inappropriate on the tenth or twentieth date, it is probably not out of lack of an interested audience. It is doubtful that many girls take these dicta programmatically, shaping their emotions and behavior to fit prior notions of acceptable progression. Few girls, however, are unaware of the implications of timing for reputation whether or not they employ it as a source of control over reputation. Because emotions are somewhat less impulsive than we generally prefer to believe, being sponsored and shaped by a social context, it is no surprise to find emotions arising spontaneously in the very circumstances we would rationally require.

The final two patterns have less to do with dating and sexual experience generally, and more to do with the specific issue of sexual intercourse and the specific concerns of more sexually experienced girls.[2] The concerns which make sense of the maintenance of technical virginity and the structured use of contraceptive methods are, however, simply extensions of the concerns with self-respect and reputation which characterize less permissive stages of sexual involvement.

2. I have used the phrase "sexually experienced" as a shorthand way of referring to girls who have had sexual intercourse. It is meant neither pejoratively nor offhandedly.

There is a great deal of evidence that many girls who do not view sexual intercourse as acceptable, nevertheless accept every activity up to that point—including genital stimulation and genital apposition. Ehrmann observes, for his sample, that of the girls who had gone beyond light petting (about one-third had), "a majority . . . had indulged in all heterosexual practices except actual intercourse" (1960 : 57). Without longitudinal evidence it is difficult to determine how long most girls accept heavy petting without accepting sexual intercourse as well. It is clear, however, that heavy petting is not experienced by girls as simply a temporary prelude to the acceptance of intercourse, but as a clear stage of sexual activity which may operate as an ultimate standard over some time, perhaps until marriage. It is currently fashionable, and perhaps accurate, to view the symbolic value attached to virginity in its most technical sense as rationally ridiculous, engendering habits and frustrations which later prove unsuitable to marital sexuality and which, in the meantime, observe no more than the technicalities of one morality. But, from the point of view of a girl who is ambivalent, the maintenance of technical virginity protects one definition of herself and her behavior. Attempts and intents to preserve virginity have a moral legitimacy which may be lessened but not eradicated if the attempt rests on a technicality and the intent is born of nervousness.

Heavy petting, however, comes perilously close to sexual intercourse and creates the risk of pregnancy—a risk which is not likely to be acknowledged or provided for by the girl who defines herself as a virgin.

Contraceptive Use

Virtually no studies of premarital sexual behavior have made any systematic inquiry into the contraceptive practices of the sexually experienced young. These studies usually view sexual intercourse as the ultimate stage of a premarital sexual career, and implicitly treat contraception as a kind of technical decision which follows on the fear of pregnancy.

Yet there is reason to suspect that contraception is not so rational, so technical, so automatic a matter. In a recent and excellent study of premarital sexual behavior among British teen-agers—the only source of systematic evidence about contraception among the unmarried—Schofield (1965 : 111) makes the following sober observation:

> The girls have a very real fear of pregnancy and yet they do almost nothing to take precautions. In the whole sample 82 per cent said they knew something about the sort of precautions people take to avoid pregnancy, and yet only three (less than 0.5 per cent) girls had ever bought a contraceptive and nearly all the experienced girls left it to the boy to decide what form of birth control he would use, if any.

Even among the married, for whom sexual relations are not conflicted by moral prohibition against intercourse, contraceptive use is not merely a technical decision requiring only facts, money, and accessibility of some technique. Each contraceptive method makes some requirements of the relationship within which it is used and expresses some aspects of sexuality to its users. Feelings about sexuality, about the possibility of control over one's life, conceptions of male and female responsibilities, the ease with which a husband and wife can talk about sexual matters—these are the conditions within which contraceptive use must take place (Rainwater 1966; 1970).

Contraceptive use is less a technical decision than a concern which has a number of emotional, moral, and social significances for its users. For the unmarried, these significancies are shaped by the prohibitions and moral ambivalences surrounding premarital sexual experience.

If we look at premarital sexual experience rather than simply at behavior, there is good reason to suspect that the stages of sexual experience do not simply wind up in the transition from heavy petting to sexual intercourse. Rather, there are several stages of sexual experience beyond heavy petting which cannot be lumped together under the rubric *sexual intercourse.* These stages are differentiated in terms of the acceptance of sexuality, and these degrees of acceptance are expressed and symbolized in contraceptive practices. In some anticipation of the argument, these stages occur in the following sequence. In her initial experiences with sexual intercourse, a girl will leave the matter of contraception up to her boyfriend who may or may not take adequate measures to avoid pregnancy. Taking contraceptive precautions of her own may follow this first stage and probably requires a long-term sexual involvement in which the boy supports and organizes her attempt to acquire contraceptive means. Ultimately a girl may be contraceptively prepared outside of and regardless of a specific love relationship.

In maternity homes I have heard parents and staff members express the view that it is the *good* girls who get pregnant—the girls who don't know enough, aren't experienced enough to take contraceptive precautions. In this remark there is kindness, a preferred version of the past, and only a partial truth. Both ignorance and innocence are complex and subtle matters involving preferred views of the self, shades of moral intent, practical relevancies and special evasions— matters which do not reduce to questions of factual knowledge and right behavior.

If there is truth to the *good girl* defense, it lies less in questions of information and experience than in the recognition that unconcern with contraception can express and symbolize *innocence* or at least good intentions. On the one hand, moral and reputational ambivalence about sexual intercourse does not sponsor rationality about contraception— in this sense, contraceptive devices or plans express an intent which girls may prefer to evade. I have argued that increasing permissiveness in the course of a girl's sexual career is made possible by culturally supported evasions which neutralize internal disapproval and allow a girl to sustain a view of herself as respectable. Evasion of intent may operate as a kind of prerequisite for sexual intercourse initially. Schofield's observation that much sexual experience among young people occurs without any contraception supports this view.[3]

On the other hand, contraceptive preparation is made difficult because it is symbolic of sexual intention and sophistication not just to the girl herself but to others—including the boys she dates. No amount of modesty or genuine sexual innocence can redeem the implications of, for example, possessing a diaphragm or taking birth-control pills. In this sense, contraceptive preparation is a reputational matter—a self-definitional matter which transcends moral intentions and private evasions.[4] Even the girl who accepts sexual intercourse for herself may be reluctant to express her acceptance in so tangible a way, particularly when the acquisition of contraceptive means requires contact with others.

Out of frustration at the lack of evidence about the contraceptive practices and concerns of unmarried girls, I carried

3. Schofield (1965 : 107) reports that 61 per cent of the sexually experienced girls in his sample had never used a birth-control method. As reported by those girls who had used some contraceptive means, the methods which were used were largely ones for which the boy was responsible: sheath (78 per cent), withdrawal (40 per cent), safe period (19 per cent), diaphragm (14 per cent).

It is also worth noting that of the 57 single women included in Nancy Lee's (1969) study of abortion, most of whom were in their twenties, 23 were involved in a relationship in which contraceptive methods were not used. Contraceptive nonuse does not therefore appear to be a specialty only of the young, or, as has occasionally been argued, of girls who become unwed mothers.

4. This has been recognized explicitly with respect to unwed mothers by Bowerman, Irish, and Pope (1963–1966), who observe, as the concluding section of their study, that, given the difficulties of effective contraceptive preparation, "it really isn't at all difficult to become an unwed mother" (393).

out an interview study of about half the girls at a small, co-ed, liberal arts college. In the remainder of this section, material from this small study is used to illustrate the speculations I have made regarding the contraceptive concerns of girls as they become more sexually permissive.

Because of the nature of the college and of the students it recruits, this material represents one extreme of premarital sexual experience. The college is experimental and recruits students who are interested in its unconventionality. In addition the college has dispensed with much of the usual paraphernalia which symbolizes and enforces sexual restraint. There are no separate rules governing girls, no enforced hours, no rigid segregation of the sexes in housing, and no enforced restriction on cross-sex visiting in rooms. The college therefore allows a much greater amount of sexual freedom than most colleges. Furthermore, the student atmosphere is highly tolerant of premarital sexual relations, and the student culture virtually proselytizes for *rationality about sex*—that is, for contraceptive use. If we find contraception to be not simply a technical decision but a decision with moral, emotional, reputational, and self-definitional implications in this setting, then surely these implications will be magnified for most girls who, if they become involved in sexual intercourse, must do so in settings which are a good deal less supportive.

A full description of the selection of interviewees and the method of interviewing is provided at the end of the book. It is worth noting here that no attempt was made to interview only sexually experienced girls, although most girls interviewed were in fact experienced. Thirty-six of the fifty-one girls interviewed had had sexual intercourse; twelve of the fifteen inexperienced girls were freshmen—which perhaps testifies to one influence of college. It is the experience of the thirty-six that is of concern here.

The concerns of those girls who are *not* currently using a self-provided means of contraception are quite clearly reputational and self-definitional ones; these girls prefer to rely on the boy and feel constrained about acquiring contraceptive means by the self-definitional implications of doing so, as well as by their uncertainty and sense of potential embarrassment.

> . . . besides, going on the pill seems like a pretty sinful thing to do for some reason. It's like admitting something. . . . I still like to fool myself into thinking I'm a good little girl who doesn't sleep with boys and such. I never thought about the whole thing and talked about it. I haven't thought about it much . . . [later] I don't tell people I'm not a virgin. I'd just as soon people don't know that about me. I avoid talking about it with anyone, unless they have some reason to know.
>
> [How did you happen to consider using foam?]
> I remember the first time I used it. A guy bought me some, so I used it.
> [Did you know he was going to get it?]
> We had talked about it before that. I didn't expect him to have it that night.
> [How did you feel when he presented you with it?]
> I think I hesitated at first, but I was easily convinced I should use it.[5]

❀   ❀   ❀

> [Are there some methods of contraception you have considered using but haven't for one reason or another?]
> I've always kind of been tempted to use the pill, but I didn't want to walk into a doctor's office and pretend I was married, or go in and just say I want an examination and the pills. . . . I guess the only other contraceptive I've been tempted with is walking into a drugstore and seeing jelly

5. Quotes from separate girls are separated by asterisks. Each quote in this chapter comes from a different girl.

and cream. I thought I could just get some and walk up to the druggist and buy some. But then I thought I didn't want the druggist to know what I wanted it for, which he would. . . . I thought maybe you had to be married to buy some, but I guess they wouldn't do that. I just sort of concluded I didn't want it that badly. . . . I guess this all boils down to—I suppose this is kind of wrong, but I'm comfortable with it—I figure it ought to be up to the boy. I guess it's because the first boy I went with always had a condom. I didn't know anything about contraceptives. If Allen could walk into a drugstore and get a condom, I ought to be able to walk in and get jelly. I guess it's more accepted of the boys.

These concerns may also prevent a girl who is not currently involved in a sexual relationship from anticipating involvement by being contraceptively prepared—even if she has been involved in such a relationship previously and favors contraceptive use.

[Are there some methods of contraception you have considered using but haven't for one reason or another?]

Pills. It's just me—I'm not really sure why. I don't like to be labeled as one who takes pills. If I were using them, I wouldn't let it be known. My morals are high, but I have changed since I came here. I don't look down on anyone who takes them—that's their choice. It might be a different story if I were involved. To me, if I weren't going with someone and was taking pills, it would be like advertising that I'm an easy make. I also think that it would really mess me up emotionally. If I was taking pills and was confronted with a boy, I might sleep with him without really wanting to. I'd start condemning myself. . . .

[You said your views have changed?]

Yes. People here are much different than those I knew

at home. People are much more relaxed and take life as it is. People at home gossiped and that was all they had. In fact if I do get involved with someone, I would take pills.

By contrast with these girls, however, the contraceptive preparation of the others is striking. Twenty-seven of the thirty-six sexually experienced girls used either the pill or coil. What is even more striking, however, is the extent to which contraceptive preparation is related to coming to college—to this particular college. While girls who began sexual relations in college almost invariably use the pill or coil (seventeen out of eighteen), girls who began sexual relations before coming to college have not typically used these methods until they came to college; of the fifteen girls who had sexual relations before college, ten currently use the pill or coil, but only three of these had used these methods prior to college.[6] I read these facts to say that contraceptive preparation goes less with involvement in sexual relations than with acceptance of that involvement—an acceptance which, in the case of these girls, is promoted by the college atmosphere. This reading is borne out by these girls' own understandings of their change in contraceptive practice.

[How did you happen to consider using foam?]
I didn't consider it at all. One time I thought *he* would have prophylactics and he didn't—he had foam. I used it improperly as a matter of fact. . . .
[How did you feel about using it the first time?]
Pretty odd. There were no instructions on how to use it. I don't know if I got it in the right place. I had to run off to the bathroom and perform the magical rites.
[How did you happen to consider the pill?]

6. For three of the thirty-six experienced girls, some information was either ambiguous or missing; their experience is therefore not included in these figures.

I was always going to use it but I didn't want to. My roommate had one or two months' supply which she'd stolen from her father who is a gynecologist. Since I didn't have to go to the doctor I sort of eased into taking them and after two months I decided to go to the doctor, since pills were so much easier to use. . . .

[Could you compare it to before you took the pill?]

I definitely felt more in control. No longer would it have to be discussed. I wouldn't have to rely on the boy. It was admitting to needing the pill. Before, even the idea that I was the kind of girl that needed to take the pill was too outrageous . . . less the thirteen-year-old with the suave, older man saying, "Don't tell me you're not on the pill, you sweet young thing." I feel older, a lot less nervous. Now I could devote some energy to my feelings about the boy. . . . To not take the pill I'm merely a bad little girl. It's being pretty fugitive, while taking the pill is a positive decision.

＊　　＊　　＊

[Was there a difference between high school and now?]

Yes. In high school maybe we didn't use contraceptives fifty per cent of the time—well, maybe one per cent without *any* (referring to rhythm). . . .

[How did you happen to use foam?]

My boyfriend took me to the drugstore and told me to go in and buy foam. I didn't like it. It was very awkward. People were watching and I didn't know which to buy. I was also resentful because he wouldn't come in with me. I didn't like using foam at all. I didn't know at what point in petting I should use it, should I go in the bathroom. I was really uptight about it. . . .

[Would you say your feelings regarding using contraceptive techniques have changed in any way since you first engaged in sexual relations?]

Yes. Now contraception is matter of fact. Sex in high school was entirely different. I was ridden with guilt and secrecy, plus it was hard to get contraceptives. Here (at the college) use of them is a basic assumption. There is nothing hidden. I'm not afraid to talk with girls about it now, whereas in high school—God, if I had ever talked to anybody!

For those girls who became involved in sexual relations only after coming to college, much of the ambivalence about sexual relations, and therefore about contraception, is attenuated by the open support for both at this college. In this atmosphere, a girl need not depend on her boyfriend to support and organize her attempts to acquire contraceptive protection. She finds among her friends a number who will provide her with information, names, and support necessary to get any method of contraception; in fact, her friends may actually make the doctor's appointment, take her there, and see that she gets the prescription filled.

It is therefore interesting that even in this atmosphere of remarkable support that girls still report having to come to terms with sexual relations and with the self-defining implications of contraceptive preparation before they are able to protect themselves adequately against possible pregnancy.

[How did you feel using foam?]
Wicked. Because I had never used any contraceptive devices before.
[But you had relations before?]
Yeah.
[Then why did you feel wicked?]
It was like sort of a step up into the big time. It also felt medical. I guess because of all the paraphernalia involved. It was like saying "I'm having sex and I'm being very conscious and rational about it all." And it's like something

you've read about and heard people talk about, and all of a sudden there I was doing the same thing and putting myself in the same kind of category.

[Are you implying you really didn't want to see yourself in that category?]

No, not at all. I mean, I thought it was neat, sort of worldly, I guess.

[How did you feel at the doctor's, getting the pill?]

Nervous as hell. The physical examination bothered me. I just don't like doctors at all. And not knowing what he was going to ask me. Like if he was going to ask me, "Do you love the person?" or "Why do you want pills?" I didn't know how much morality was going to be involved.

✷ ✷ ✷

[Would you say your feelings regarding using contraceptive techniques have changed since the time you first engaged in sexual relations?]

Yes. I think I kind of felt that by using contraception I was committing myself about being a certain kind of person, and about sex and intercourse. But later I began to realize that it was really more a matter of practicality than anything else.

For a girl to be explicitly concerned with the question of contraception, it is necessary that she accept a view of herself as sexually experienced and sexually knowledgeable. For reasons which have to do with the uneasy moral climate surrounding premarital sexual experience and with her own uncertainty and ambivalence, few girls will have this view of themselves on making the transition from heavy petting to sexual intercourse.

As she becomes increasingly sexually involved in what appears to her to be a long-term relationship, she is more able to view herself as experienced; furthermore, she can rely on her boyfriend to suggest contraceptive methods. Most girls, including those who have not yet participated in full sexual relations, expressed the view that a long-term relationship requires use of either the pill or the coil.

In a setting not so supportive of premarital sexual relations as this college, a long-term love relationship which is viewed as a prelude to marriage may in fact be a necessary internal justification for acquiring pills or some other self-provided means of contraception. Some cursory evidence for this is provided by a set of five interviews done by a student at Radcliffe College. She reports (Anschuetz, 1967 : 21) that the girls she interviewed had to undergo questioning by the doctors they consulted in order to obtain pills. She states:

> It is interesting that the presence of love is the main point of justification for the doctor as well as for the girl. All sensed that once they had convinced the doctor that their affair was not a fleeting infatuation but was love for which they felt responsibilities, they had his consent. Especially for those who were somewhat insecure about their action, the transformation from embarrassment to a crystallization of her position in front of the doctor was an important step.

The principled use of contraception in anticipation of possible and not necessarily long-term relationships—for example, the decision to continue taking pills after the breaking up of a long-term relationship—defines a final stage of premarital sexual experience, a stage which must be preceded by the stages already described. The girls at this stage are, sociologically speaking, principled deviants who possess a rationale, an ideology, which finds sexual relations normal and desirable and contraception practical. Even these girls who are essentially rid of ambivalence, however, express some regard for the societal climate in which they hold their views, and have some concern for impression-management. For example, several of the girls at this stage who were interviewed said they were careful away from campus about letting others know they took pills.

PREGNANCY

The major point I have wished to make is that contraceptive awareness and preparation on the part of unmarried girls is likely to be minimal at the stage of transition between heavy petting and sexual intercourse. I have dwelt on the problems of self-respect and moral ambivalence which are raised at each transition to a more permissive stage of sexual experience—problems which are handled by culturally derived evasions and techniques of neutralizing internal disapproval. Unconcern with contraception is such a technique for it allows a girl to evade recognition of what she is doing and to sustain a preferred view of herself.

There is another sense, however, in which unconcern with contraception is not merely subjectively handy but is also objectively sensible. A girl who is unconcerned with contraception risks pregnancy, but this risk is reduced if her boyfriend is responsible and if sexual intercourse is an intermittent rather than a regular experience. A girl who is contraceptively prepared, however, risks the imputation of promiscuity and a damaged reputation. A girl who, in some measure, still adheres to a standard that excludes sexual intercourse may prefer the risk of possible pregnancy to the more probably risk of loss of reputation.

Until there is more evidence, much of this must be speculation. If it is true, however, that contraceptive concern is least likely during the transition between heavy petting and sexual intercourse, then illegitimate pregnancy is less a product of the psychological makeup of particular girls and more a product of a particular stage of sexual experience. Becoming pregnant out of wedlock is interpreted, following this analysis, as the incidental by-product of choosing not to concern oneself with contraception, and this choice is linked to one stage of a typical sexual career.[7]

The interesting consequence may therefore be that commitment to conventional moral standards controls and structures deviant activity—increasing sexual involvement—but that this commitment may also be the way in which the most deviant results are produced. It is in this sense that the dictum, "Don't do it, but if you do, be careful," is a particularly silly recommendation, for it is precisely the feeling that sexual intercourse is not a morally desirable alternative that makes contraceptive preparation unlikely.

Following this analysis, a girl who finds herself unexpectedly pregnant is likely to be a girl who has been able to maintain a definition of herself as essentially conventional, virtuous, nonpromiscuous despite her participation in sexual activity about which she may feel vaguely or explicitly unconfortable. When she finds herself pregnant, the problem she faces is that this definition of herself is severely jeopardized.

The study reported in the chapters to follow has to do with the experiences of girls who did not solve this problem in the most typical ways—by abortion or marriage—but became unwed mothers in the temporary care of a maternity home.

7. In these paragraphs I have essentially applied to illegitimate pregnancy a paradigm used by Strodtbeck, Short, and Cartwright in their discussions of delinquency and unmarried fatherhood (Short, Strodtbeck, and Cartwright, 1962; Short and Strodtbeck, 1965; Strodtbeck and Short, 1964). They suggest that it is useful to make the distinction between acts with some origin in deviant motivation and those which can be more rightly considered the incidental by-product risked in undertaking other acts less deviant than their aleatory (independent) outcome. They argue persuasively that young lower-class males may risk violence in order to "join the action" and maintain status and may risk paternity in the process of gaining status from sexual exploits. The "aleatory risk" approach has the advantage of not conferring false motivations-to-deviance and of respecting the calculus according to which the risk may be worth taking.

The central feature of these girls' moral careers as unwed mothers is the experience of coming to realign themselves with the conventional, respectable world;[8] the central theme of this book has to do with the ways in which maternity homes sponsor and organize this experience of moral realignment.

8. It is relevant to the concerns of this chapter to remark in advance that girls may, in fact, be realigned to the very concerns and stage of sexual activity in which pregnancy is maximally risked.

2

Becoming an Unwed Mother

The stigmatized individual tends to hold the same beliefs about identity that we do . . . the standards he has incorporated from the wider society equip him to be intimately alive to what others see as his failing, inevitably causing him, if only for moments, to agree that he does indeed fall short of what he really ought to be. Shame becomes a central possibility, arising from the individual's perception of one of his own attributes as being a defiling thing to possess, and one he can readily see himself as not possessing.

ERVING GOFFMAN
Stigma (1963 : 7)

From this point on I will be drawing primarily on my observations of two settings for unwed mothers and of the experiences of the girls who passed through them in the several months I spent at each place. These places—one a day school for young and pregnant Negro girls, the other a residential maternity home attracting a more middle-class and white clientele—will be referred to, respectively, as the Project and

Hawthorne House. Interviews at a third setting, to be called Kelman Place, will be used as supplementary material.[1]

While the chapters which follow have to do with the experience of becoming an unwed mother at the Project and at Hawthorne House, this chapter has to do with girls' experiences before arriving at either place. It is these prior experiences which conditioned the girls' initial reactions to the institutions and, to a large extent, these prior experiences made it possible for the institutions to take a forgiving and sheltering stance toward their clients.

I therefore wish to delay introducing the settings further and instead call upon the girls' recollections to describe their concerns upon finding themselves pregnant, and to comment more generally on the process of arriving at some solution to the problem of an illegimate pregnancy.

THE ALTERNATIVES

The girl who finds herself illegitimately pregnant is faced with a limited number of alternatives—abortion, marriage, or having an illegitimate child she may or may not keep. Because the alternatives are so few and so seemingly obvious, it is tempting to assume that pregnant girls make a choice among these alternatives, a choice which reflects certain preferences, certain values.

It is commonly argued, for example, that the less frequent choice of abortion and marriage among lower-class Negroes indicates the greater moral acceptability of illegitimacy in Negro lower-class culture. The choice of abortion or marriage is seen as a choice for respectability; if Negro girls do

1. The names of these settings have been altered in agreement with the conditions I set for myself in requesting permission to observe them. In the cases of Hawthorne House and Kelman Place, this disguise was explicitly requested by the staff. The Project which is more unusual is more thinly disguised.

not make that choice, then illegitimacy must be not so unrespectable in black circles.[2] This view is, of course, not a purely neutral speculation. It is very rarely argued, for example, that Negro girls are willing to lose a more difficultly maintained social esteem in order to be mothers to their children while middle-class white girls are not willing to go that far despite their commitment to the same value.

With as little evidence as there is, however, it is difficult to imagine correctly the choices pregnant girls experience themselves as making, or what these choices represent to the girls involved. The experiences of the young, lower-class, and Negro Project girls serve as an illustration.

For the Project girls, obtaining an abortion did not exist as an alternative. There were of course good realistic reasons why these girls would not get abortions. Obtaining an abortion requires financial, social, and psychological resources not possessed by fourteen-year-old girls. Even aside from these reasons, however, the Project girls did not appear to be aware of this sort of abortion as a possibility. Whenever abortion was mentioned spontaneously or in answer to a question of mine, girls spoke only in terms of self-induced abortion and the dangers involved.

Marriage did exist as an alternative for many of these girls, although their youth would have made parental consent necessary and perhaps less likely. Yet for the Project girls marriage had a quite different meaning than it does for middle-class girls, and their "choice" of illegitimacy can only be understood in terms of this meaning.

For the Project girls, marriage was not something they could realistically count on to be a reasonably happy and long-term arrangement. If marriage generally represents

2. This argument is presented, for example, by Robert R. Bell in his review of the literature dealing with premarital sexual relations among Negroes, In *Premarital Sex in a Changing Society* (Englewood Cliffs, N.J.: Prentice-Hall, 1966), pp. 118–123.

respectability, in their eyes, it was at best an uncertain and easily jeopardized respectability. While many of the Hawthorne House and Kelman Place girls expressed reservations about getting married to a particular boy, under the particular circumstances, the Project girls' reservations had to do with marriage in general. To them, marriage meant resignation at a very early age to a way of life which included a limitation on freedom, increased responsibility, trouble, more children, and the possibility of abandonment.

I didn't want to get married. If I get married, all you do is bring more babies in the house. So I thought I would take it the hard way.

MARIANNE[3]

*   *   *

I didn't want to get married. I wouldn't mind when I'm older. But I want to finish school. . . . I ain't ready for no husband. I like to sleep. I don't want to be fixing no breakfast, fixing no lunch—I'm not used to all that stuff. If I get married there be many a day with nothing cooked, and he be getting mad and we be fighting. I don't want to have no husband at a young age like I am right now.

MAY

*   *   *

[How do people react when you say you're going to get married?]

Some say "I'm not going to have no man beat on me every day." They got boyfriends who do that. Their boyfriend catch them with another boy and pow right in the eye. . . .

3. Girls' names have been altered consistently so that the same name identifies the same girl throughout the book. My own questions appear in brackets.

[What do they think marriage is like?]

That you do what he say, stay in the house, cook. I say if you marry a man you 'posed to cook and stay home some, but not all the time. And they think it's beating. With my boyfriend, he raise his voice and I know he means business. Once I started to smoke and he told me he didn't like it so I stopped. He didn't have to pop me in no eye. . . .

[Would you say girls look forward to marriage?]

They don't look forward to it. They probably think different when they get older.

Rowena

There was another sense too in which not getting married allowed girls to hold out hopes for a more respectable life. An illegitimate pregnancy jeopardized more than moral respectability for these girls; it lessened their chances for continuing in school and possibly attaining a better way of life. Marriage was seen by many Project girls and their parents as more an obstacle than a solution to this other sort of respectability. As one girl put it:

Some of these girls around here just don't think ahead. They think they'll get married and leave school and they don't think that maybe their husband won't stay around and then where will they be when they can't do anything. Some of them don't even graduate from grammar school. What kind of mother could you be not even out of grammar school? If your kid has work from school, you can't even help him, maybe can't even read. At least that's one thing I've learned. When I got pregnant, my mother talked to me. She told me that everybody's ship is going to come in sometime, but that you had to be there when it came 'cause you can only get it once. She said I was only part

way up the gangplank. I think it is foolish to get married
with so much ahead of you.

BELINDA

In other words, middle-class girls could view marriage as
a solution to the problem of an illegitimate pregnancy in a
way that these girls realistically could not. The Project girls'
choice had less to do with the moral acceptability or attract-
iveness of illegitimacy and more to do with the facts of
lower-class life for Negroes in this society.[4]

It is less easy to interpret the "choice" of illegitimacy by the
girls who came to Hawthorne House and Kelman Place, in
part because illegitimacy is a less usual solution for middle-
class girls. Without knowing more about the circumstances,
concerns, and steps which lead to marriage or abortion, it is
difficult to know what the less usual choice of illegitimacy
represents, or even to what extent it can be considered a
choice.

Becoming pregnant is a situation which few girls seem to
envision happening to themselves and for which girls are
remarkably ill-prepared. The most difficult and most real
fact about illegitimate pregnancy for most girls is that each
alternative is extremely undesirable and the grounds for
determining which is the lesser evil unclear.[5]

4. This argument has been more extensively and more theoretically
made by Lee Rainwater (1966; 1970). Using evidence from his study
of the Pruitt-Igoe housing project in St. Louis, Rainwater critically
discusses the notion that the values which govern lower-class Negro
attitudes toward marriage and illegitimacy are somehow different
from those of the larger society.

Elliot Liebow has described similarly the conditions which make
stable marriage and the raising of children a difficult and ambiva-
lently viewed experience among lower-class Negro men (Liebow,
1966; 1967).

5. In response to Schofield's (1965 : 110) question, "What would
you do if you were going to have a baby?", girls arrayed themselves
in the following order: tell my parents, try to marry the father, make

It is in relation to this initial quandary that revealing the situation to others becomes important. For while each solution must eventually involve revealing her situation to some others, telling appears to be more than a matter of informing, more than a matter of asking for information. The process of talking with others helps to transform uncertainty into preference.

Of the three solutions to the problem of pregnancy, abortion probably comes closest to being an individual choice, for it requires a relatively swift decision and a certain amount of disciplined information-seeking. Yet in a recent study of how women reach an abortionist (the volunteers were educated, middle-class women in their early twenties), only about half were fairly determined to acquire an abortion from the time pregnancy was first suspected. About half developed their intention in the process of talking with others (Lee, 1965 : 53–57).

The process of talking with others has the consequence of organizing not only information and preferences, but also the grounds for evaluating the possible alternatives.

As an illustration, the girl quoted below had unsuccessfully tried to get an abortion, and was, at the time of the interview, living with relatives and making arrangements to have her baby adopted. The interview excerpt conveys her initial gratitude to her boyfriend and his parents for their financial support for an abortion, and her shift to resentment that they had not acted as she later learned parents ought to act.

---

arrangements to keep it, try to have it adopted, get rid of it. Their responses suggest that abstractly, that is, normatively, marriage is the most acceptable solution, while abortion is the least acceptable. Whatever abstract conceptions a girl may have, however, pale in the actuality of having to marry a particular boy at a particular time, of having to find an abortionist, or of having to plan realistically for a child.

My mother absolutely didn't have any idea what to do [said with astonishment]. It was like she couldn't figure out whether to bawl me out or sort of sit down and cry or something. I told her she should try to get me an abortion. She did work trying to find me one.

[How did she go about that?]

We went to the family doctor who is a real fuddy-duddy. All he said was that I should get married and tell the boy's parents. My mother thought that was a simply marvelous idea. At that point I didn't think it was fair to have his parents told.

[I thought they already knew because of the money they sent for an abortion.]

By that time Jim had already told them that I had gotten the abortion. Actually I was surprised that they had given him the money so quickly. As a matter of fact, I was taken back at the time but I didn't know why. Then when I saw that in my neighborhood when this sort of thing happens the parents get together and they get married. . . .

[How is that?]

I kept hearing about these things and some of them worked out well. That's what the parents always do, which is why the doctor said to tell his parents. Most parents wouldn't want their son's girlfriend to have an abortion, that's all. My mother kept saying that if my brother had ever been in a situation like this, she would have been sure that he'd gotten married. And I think that it would have happened in most instances. but I didn't know all this at the time when Jim got the money.

While telling others therefore focuses the practical issue of what to do, it also focuses the moral or self-definitional issues which are raised by the situation of pregnancy. For the girls who came to the Project, Hawthorne House, and Kelman Place, the anticipation and act of telling others, particularly parents, defined the first stages of their moral careers as unwed mothers. And their experiences are in some measure the initial experiences of girls who arrive at other solutions to the problem of pregnancy.

Telling Others

Previously protected by a version of herself as an essentially respectable girl, the girl who finds herself pregnant faces the unexpected prospect of seeing herself as the kind of girl who gets pregnant. In the solitude of her growing suspicion that she is pregnant, and in her growing panic as time and the limited possibilities force private awareness toward revelation, she anticipates the likely reactions of others and appreciates that it is a view of her self that is at stake.

It is perhaps evidence for the thesis presented in the preceding chapter that very few of these girls took advantage of the defensive possibilities in their situation—for example, to maintain that premarital sexual activity is acceptable and that getting pregnant is a practical, not moral, trouble. Uncommitted to her own sexual behavior, the girl who finds herself pregnant is ready to disavow the past. In anticipating the reactions of others, particularly those of her parents and those of a more diffusely conceived public, she prepares to agree with any moral reevaluation which may be made of her behavior and of the kind of person she has been.

She begins to apply to herself what she imagines to be the public typification of an illegitimately pregnant girl. The experience of trying out this other version of herself, of practicing seeing herself as others do not yet see her, is the first moral experience in the career of the illegitimately pregnant girl.

Louise asked during group meeting, "Can you remember what you thought of unwed mothers in places like this before? I mean, think of what we thought, before we came here, about unwed mothers and maternity homes."

Peg said, "That's right. Whenever I thought of places like this, I always thought, 'Well, I'm not that type of girl.' " Everyone looked agreeing to this.

(Hawthorne House[6])

*   *   *

[Did you go back to your other school after reading about the Project school in the paper?]

No, I didn't want to go back. I stayed at home for about two weeks. I knew the way it would be with talking and whispering to each other and everything. . . . I was just trying to keep it from them as long as possible. I was ashamed of it I guess.

[What would happen if they knew?]

They wouldn't be nice things. Look at that little whore —she be pregnant. They probably think you were fast or something. I don't know what else. They just talk about you. . . .

[What does *fast* mean?]

They say a girl is fast, they mean she goes around with boys, she smokes, she drinks.

[Do you think they will talk when you go back?]

They might not if you try to change. If you continue to go to school and stay off streets. Like now I stay home till my boyfriend comes to take me for a ride. But if they

6. A comment must be made here about the format of quotes as they appear through the rest of the book. Quotes from Kelman Place come from interviews. Quotes dealing with Hawthorne House were obtained through participant-observation and come from field notes. The format expresses this difference in method. Quotes from the Project come both from interviews and from participant-observation, and are therefore presented in a somewhat more confusing way. Yet I have generally tried to preserve, through format, some sense of how the encounter occurred and especially of the part I played in it.

see you hanging on the same corner, and smoking and drinking.

JOALANA (The Project)

*   *   *

Also there was a girl near us who was eighteen and she had a baby, and my uncle was constantly saying things about her. He get to talking so much about her and it would make me irritable. It was *nerve*wracking.

[How come?]

It was as if he was trying to see if I was, or what I'd do. I would get up and walk out of the room, and if I stayed there, I tell him not to talk about it.

MARIANNE (The Project)

*   *   *

[Is having a baby common, would you say, at your school?]

Lots of kids over at my school are having babies.

[How did you feel about them before it happened to you?]

I say you should be ashamed of yourself. Now I be saying it to myself.

MAY (The Project)

*   *   *

During a private discussion with Dale in the sitting room, she said at one point, "But you know, when you first get pregnant, you think 'Oh no, not me. I'm not that type of girl.' "

(Hawthorne House)

The most striking feature of the girls' accounts of their first experiences on finding themselves pregnant is the extent to which they expect far more severe moral reactions from others than they typically experience.

On the one hand, expecting the worst tends to defuse the explosive possibilities of others' reactions. For example, the mood in which girls anticipate telling their parents, which for most girls was one of the most difficult moments in their careers as unwed mothers, is a mood in which almost any actual reaction is preferably to the extremes of imagination which run to the formulas of bad fiction—being thrown out, killed, heart attacks. The mood of confession and contrition with which most girls approach those who would evaluate their behavior makes moralizing unnecessary, gratuitous.

On the other hand, the public view of the girl who is pregnant out of wedlock is more charitable, and offers more alternative views of her behavior and her self than the girl at first expects. While getting pregnant though unmarried is not viewed amiably, a relatively young girl, pregnant for the first time, is more likely to be looked at as worthy of pity and help than of scorn and derision. The old-fashioned image of the girl led astray and forsaken by her lover is, surprisingly enough, still not far from the latent conception of the unwed mother in the public mind. Given the right evidence of demeanor, emotion, and possibly status, a girl will be classified as this sort of nice girl who made a mistake, a mistake which is punishment enough in itself, and the lesson to be learned will be viewed as so obvious that it does not need stressing. She will be viewed as in need of seclusion and support rather than of rehabilitation; her repentance and reformation will be taken for granted.

The particular way in which sex education is repeatedly linked with the problem of unwed mothers illustrates the way the same fundamental conception of the unwed mother underlies a seemingly more sophisticated concern.

Unwed mothers are popularly viewed as a justification for the spread of sex education programs, as well as a logical group to study in the development of such programs. During the several months I spent at Hawthorne House, for example, the topic of sex education came up a number of times. A number of girls participated in a series of discussions of their sex education programs—portions were taped and sent to the person who had requested the information.

Implicit in this link of sex education programs, as they are usually conceived and executed, to unwed mothers is the view that sex education somehow will prevent illegitimate pregnancies by preventing premarital sexual relations. It is rarely argued, except in the more avant-garde circles, that girls get pregnant because they have not had adequate instruction or sanction in the use of contraceptive methods. The bafflement felt when education fails to answer what is a moral not informational question is expressed with most impact in the words of a mother at a parents' meeting at Hawthorne House.

"But I told my daughter everything, and still this happened. I explained it all to her and said that she should wait until after marriage. I couldn't have told her more, and yet this happened." She began crying.

The man at the front said, "Yes, we wonder where we did fail."

Whether expressed in the more old-fashioned notion of a *mistake* which was probably the result of being "fast-talked by some boy" or in the more modern concern with sex education, the terms for understanding the situation of a pregnant girl have greater possibilities for moral reprieve than she initially anticipates—or perhaps feels she has a right to expect.

One of the major consequences therefore of the eventual disclosure of her illegitimate pregnancy is the beginning of a process whereby the anticipated and occasionally applied definition of her as a *sexually promiscuous girl* is exchanged for that of *girl in trouble,* or *unwed mother.* While the materials for this transformation exist in the public repertoire of understandings of pregnant girls, entrance into a maternity home organizes and ratifies this transformation.

ENTERING A MATERNITY HOME

As they have been traditionally conceived and operated, maternity homes have directly taken what I have called a *girl in trouble* view of their clients—the view that these are essentially respectable girls who made a mistake. Maternity homes have traditionally offered seclusion and support to girls whose wish to hide and whose intention to place their babies for adoption were taken as sufficient indication of their correct understanding of the moral order.

Maternity homes have offered not only a place to hide and a connection with adoption facilities but also moral rescue in the form of an officially expressed definition of their clients as essentially respectable. Many maternity homes, particularly those which have not yet been affected by the orientations of professional social work, not only support but officially insist on this view of their clients.

> These are your loving, trusting girls in here. Your other girl who is probably doing the same thing doesn't get caught because she is too smart. . . . What is needed is more understanding on the part of the parents and the general public. I don't mean condoning, I mean understanding . . . that this kind of thing can happen and these girls do need help. (Quoted from the Director of a Crittenton home in Florida by the *St. Petersburg Times*, May 17, 1968.)

Staff members at Kelman Place, a residence for unwed mothers run as an adjunct to an adoption agency, repeatedly stressed the moral quality of their clients.

> Actually I had originally come here just to interview people for this job for Mrs. Washburne. I had not originally intended to take the job myself. . . . We ran quite an

attractive ad. It stressed the chance to do dedicated work for a nominal salary plus room and board. It was a blind ad. There were so few people who, when they found out what the job was, wanted it. And we wanted to be selective. Some were the police type. And others just said they didn't think they would care for girls like that. It was one or the other. You should have heard them—saying they didn't care for girls like that. I said [she sounded genuinely indignant], "Our girls are not promiscuous. They have made a mistake."

Mrs. Winton (Kelman Place)

✿ ✿ ✿

Most are college girls. They are screened, of course, before they get here. We do not have promiscuous girls. If they are not college girls, they are still very refined girls. . . .

I talk a lot with the girls. In general, with the whole group I would say they know what they have done is not condoned by society and never will be—never. I do not condemn a girl for making one mistake. I just hope they learn a lesson.

Mrs. Palmer (Kelman Place)

Many of the rules of Kelman Place are designed in such a way as to express and enforce a nonpromiscuous and respectable definition of girls while they are in a situation which jeopardizes it.

You will not receive any male visitor except your father or your clergyman, and you will receive him in the living room. He is not to be introduced to other guests.

Your physician recommends a daily walk for your good health. Guests may leave the house in twos, but not in groups, nor gather outside the house in groups, such as on the beach, in restaurants, etc.

Evening engagements are made only by permission of the House Mother, and on such occasions you must be escorted from and to the door, returning not later than 9 p.m. except when in company of a member of your family.

Blue jeans, shorts, or slacks not permissible.

(Excerpts from the Kelman Place rules.)

Girls who enter maternity homes which, like Kelman Place, conceive their purpose in traditional terms are thus presented rather directly with moral reprieve as well as with the conditions on which it is granted.

However, as maternity homes have become increasingly affected by the orientations of professional social work, and as the conception of services for unwed mothers has broadened to include a wider range of problems, maternity homes have become less inclined to view their primary functions in traditional terms.

The Project and Hawthorne House, for example, represent two trends away from the traditional conception of a maternity home. The Project recruits girls who would never appear at the door of a traditional maternity home—Negro girls who will keep their babies and who live at home during pregnancy—and the Project recruits girls for a service which has only lately been provided for pregnant girls—schooling. Hawthorne House, while set up along more traditional lines as a residence for pregnant girls who typically place their babies for adoption, conceives its main function to be therapeutic rather than custodial. Although a pregnant girl may come to Hawthorne House for its traditional services, she will quickly discover that these are incidental to the staff view of what she is doing there.

Neither the Project nor Hawthorne House conceive their purpose to be moral rescue, and neither extends the kind of automatic moral reprieve offered by more traditionally conceived maternity homes. Yet these two institutions share with more traditional maternity homes some features which, in spite of official intention, offer entering girls the traditional reassurances.

The most important of these features has to do with recruitment. Maternity homes tend to recruit girls who are suitable to the transformation from *sexually promiscuous girl* to *girl in trouble,* and tend not to recruit girls who would threaten such transformation. Maternity homes recruit relatively young girls (the oldest typically in their early twenties) who have never been married and who are pregnant for the first time.

While these are the girls who are attracted to maternity homes, these are also the girls who maternity homes feel are their appropriate clients. In rules which regulate hours, overnight privileges, and appropriate visitors, and in the understanding that girls come there with parental knowledge, maternity homes express a parental orientation toward their clients which is appropriate to young girls, and which discourages older girls from applying. It is interesting that both older girls and girls pregnant for the second time were seen by a psychiatrist and discussed in a meeting of the staff.

For residential maternity homes providing the traditional services of shelter and adoption counseling, such girls are atypical and can be treated as special exceptions to the usual clientele.

Institutions like the Project, however, provide services which do not necessarily select the young, the never-married, the never-previously-pregnant. Originally the Project restricted entrance to girls in their first pregnancy. This was essentially a formality, for the Project school was initially an elementary school (through eighth grade) and did not attract girls old enough to be having a second child. As the Project expanded to include higher grades and older girls, the likelihood of getting girls in their second illegitimate pregnancy increased. The moral implications of this possible change can be read in the remarks of one of the Project girls.

Several girls were having a conversation about an ex-Project girl rumored to be pregnant again. I asked, "Will she come back here?"

Beverly said, "She can't come back here."

I said, "Why is that?"

Beverly said, "They don't let you. The first one is a mistake, and that's what this is for. After that it ain't no mistake anymore.

Girls who entered Kelman Place, Hawthorne House, and the Project found themselves among girls like themselves and, regardless of the special philosophies of each place, it was this experience that shaped the girls' initial sense of moral reprieve. For in anticipating entering a maternity home, girls did not expect what they found.

[What did you expect the school to be like?]

I thought it be like a bunch of girls gossiping and hard to make friends with. I thought it would be pitiful, period.

[How is that?]

I thought I be coming over here new and pregnant—that they find something on you to talk about.

MAY (The Project)

❋　❋　❋

I didn't expect it to be very nice. I expected it to be more like a hospital or something—like a sanitarium. I had ideas about being locked in a room with bars on the windows, and all that. . . . You think you're the only nice one that's going to be around. I expected tough, juvenile delinquent types—something rather bad like something you'd see at the state girls' home.

LEILA (Kelman Place)

❋　❋　❋

I decided I'd come over to see what it was like, and then if I liked it I'd come—and if I didn't, I wouldn't. And when

I came and saw what a beautiful place it was, it completely changed my mind—and the way the girls were and everything.

[How do you mean?]

Well, you come in and you see the girls and they all look relatively cheerful and they are all well dressed and well groomed, and they are not just slopping around crying or anything. I think that's the real thing I've gotten here. . . . When you are on the outside you think that you are the only one that's in this situation and you are inclined to be gloomy and pity yourself. And then when you come to a place like this, and you see all the other girls that are like yourself, and who are nice, that's what really helps.

MILLIE (Hawthorne House)

* * *

I was expecting more of an institutional place—with a less educated group of girls. . . . That was one reason my father had for not wanting me to go to a maternity home: "You know you're going to get thrown in with a lot of trash." But I still felt I'd like to be with people my own age.

NINA (Kelman Place)

* * *

I thought girls wasn't going to be speaking to each other. I thought they would have attitudes toward each other, that they would think one person was better than another. I thought most of the girls would be ashamed and not have anything to talk about. . . . When I went there I didn't have nothing to say. Whey they started talking to me, I started talking to them.

JOALANA (The Project)

Girls enter maternity homes expecting to confront the concrete proof of what they have become and encounter instead a reminder of what they "really" are, what they presumably have been all along. It is a reminder which is expressed most saliently upon entrance in the kinds of girls recruited by maternity homes but also in certain kinds of rules as well as in less formal expectations regarding appropriate behavior and feelings.

While tempered by newer philosophies and concerns, moral reprieve is, in large measure, inherent in the traditional services provided by maternity homes—a place to hide and a place with adoption connections. Girls who enter maternity homes generally do so with the traditional intention of returning to their former lives without external trace of their experience. Maternity homes have traditionally supported this intention. As it is expressed in the hand-out received by girls entering Kelman Place:

> When you have completed your stay at Kelman Place, you must sever your connections and not return for visiting. This is for your own good—when you leave, you close the door on your experience.

I have used Kelman Place in this chapter to exemplify the traditional purposes of maternity homes—purposes which, on the Project and at Hawthorne House, have been overlaid and superseded by newer conceptions of unwed mothers and maternity homes.

As a girl's stay lengthens on the Project or at Hawthorne House, she comes into contact with these newer conceptions of what she is doing there, and encounters qualifications on the promise of moral reprieve. She will nevertheless feel upon entering, an initial moral relief which is both the product of her experiences and fears prior to coming to the institution and the product of some features which these institutions share with more traditional maternity homes.

II

The Process of
Moral Reinstatement

3

Hawthorne House*

In the broadest sense, we believe that the criteria for acceptance into our care rests on the estimated use that the client and her family can make of the agency's services. *The criteria for acceptance is not that the girl or woman is pregnant out of wedlock.*

—from a guide to intake interviewing
for staff members at Hawthorne House

Hawthorne House was a private residential maternity home located in a residential area of a large city in the East. It was a strikingly pleasant place, surrounded by grounds and trees and furnished inside with a warm tastefulness. While girls could contact Hawthorne House in the early months of pregnancy, most did not enter the home until about two months before they were due to deliver. In the meantime, many worked and lived in nearby surburban homes through arrangements made by the Hawthorne House staff, and came to Hawthorne House occasionally for counseling or to attend

*The contents of this chapter have appeared in a slightly different form in the *American Behavioral Scientist,* November–December, 1970; pp. 219–235.

the medical clinic. In this sense, the home provided services to more than the forty to sixty girls who were in residence at any one time. Because the girls' stay in the home was relatively short, Hawthorne House, like other maternity homes, had a fairly high rate of turnover compared to that of other institutions.[1]

Hawthorne House served a predominantly, although by no means exclusively, middle-class and white clientele.[2] The girls who came there were typically in their late teens, and most gave up their babies for adoption through arrangements made in conjunction with other social agencies.[3] Most girls came there for the usual reasons—to have their babies secretly.

In addition to a house and clerical staff of about twenty persons, Hawthorne House retained the part-time and full-time services of a number of professional persons including ten social workers, several doctors who staffed the weekly medical clinic,[4] several nurses, several psychiatric consultants—one of whom has run a group-therapy program in the home for a number of years, and two teachers during school season. A number of other persons came into the home for

1. Hawthorne House houses between 300 and 400 girls a year, usually for a period of seven to eight weeks.
2. The staff were concerned to recruit a greater number of girls who would not ordinarily know about or consider a maternity home; toward this end, a number of girls came to the home referred by the Division of Child Guidance and the House offered substantial, even complete, financial defrayments to girls in need. Nevertheless, even maternity homes interested in expanding the base from which clients are drawn have difficulties because the most common sources of referral (private agencies and doctors) and the conception and usual services of maternity homes do not favor the recruitment of poor, particularly black, girls.
3. From the figures for 1966, to illustrate, 309 of the 336 babies delivered were discharged to child-planning agencies.
4. Girls actually delivered at a hospital and not in the home; however, a weekly medical clinic was run in the House, and a nurse was always available on the premises.

special purposes such as running sewing classes, exercise sessions, and religious services.

The home was effectively run, however, by the professional social-work staff, for the home was their full-time concern, and they were responsible for coordinating these various services into a coherent enterprise. The weekly social-work staff meetings served as the central location for discussion and decisions regarding general policy as well as specific problems. In other ways as well, the social workers were centrally involved and attuned to the operation of the home. Every morning the house and social-work staffs met informally for coffee and casual discussion of a variety of matters including incoming girls and special events being planned. The social-work staff met less frequently but regularly with the medical and psychiatric staffs usually to discuss the problems of particular girls. When I speak of Hawthorne House and the view of their situation which girls encountered there, therefore, I will be referring to the view of the social workers, for their views shaped the general policies and specific practices of the home.

For the girls who spent the last months of pregnancy there, several aspects of Hawthorne House shaped the experience of becoming an unwed mother. First, girls encountered an explicit and psychiatric view of their situation and themselves, a view which was expressed directly in the counseling they received and less directly in a variety of house policies and routines. Second, girls encountered a set of less explicit moral concerns which centered around the issues of respectability and becoming a mother. Third, the institutional routines of the home were aligned with the process of pregnancy in ways which made time a central dimension of the girls' lives in the home and make *career* a central concept for understanding their experiences there.[5]

5. This third aspect of the girls' encounter with the House is described in the following chapter.

THE PSYCHIATRIC VIEW

The professional staff at Hawthorne House shared a view of their clients which included these presuppositions: illegitimate pregnancy is psychologically motivated, psychologically caused: without some understanding and alteration of the psychological situation which led to pregnancy, girls are likely to get pregnant again; therefore, the central purpose of the time girls spend at Hawthorne House should be to work out some understanding of the "reasons they were there."

Professional social workers are, of course, inclined by their education and training to take a psychological view of illegitimate pregnancy, particularly among middle-class girls (Perlman, 1964), and to take a casework or therapeutic tack toward the treatment of unwed mothers. Yet, in practice, these inclinations are frequently diluted by the necessity to deal with the particular problems of particular clients and by large and transitory caseloads which make an intensive, therapeutic relationship with a client impossible. I will describe in a later chapter, for example, the situation of the Project social worker who shared a similar view of unwed mothers, but was never able to systematically convey this view to the Project girls.

At Hawthorne House, however, these conceptions of illegitimate pregnancy and unwed mothers were reinforced and refined, largely as the result of staff meetings and the central position of the social workers in running the home. Because the problems and policies raised at staff meetings received theoretically inclined attention, staff conceptions of illegitimate pregnancy and unwed mothers were continually being expressed, made explicit, available, and consistent. In this way, staff members continually reminded each other of the theoretical grounds on which even minor decisions ought to be made.

Furthermore, these professional understandings, honed on daily problems, were brought to bear on a wide variety of matters which included questions of therapeutic strategy but also included such questions as whether or not the girls' last names ought to be used in the home. The overall effect was to make the conception and treatment of unwed mothers more consistent and more systematically expressed in the policies and routines of the House.

There were two terms in particular which the staff commonly used to understand a variety of issues. These terms, *responsibility* and *denial*, both expressed the staff's general etiological view of illegitimate pregnancy and linked this view to their activities in running the home. These terms were so commonly and widely used by the staff in their understanding of the girls and in their interpretation of issues that they could be considered House themes.

RESPONSIBILITY AND DENIAL

The central import of the term *responsibility* was that girls should acknowledge the consequences of their behavior and take responsibility for those consequences as well as for the chain of events which led to them. That girls might, in some sense, prefer to gloss over their past behavior or temper the seriousness of their current situation was viewed as *denial*.

These terms had meaning both with respect to the staff's view of illegitimate pregnancy as psychologically motivated and to their view of what should happen in the counseling of their clients. That is, the staff hoped to help girls take responsibility for their situations by helping them to understand and accept the part they had played in getting pregnant.

At another level, however, these terms had meaning for the staff in relation to their conception of a maternity home.

Hawthorne House has been in existence for over forty years and during most of that time it was a protective, seclusive, and charitable hideaway for girls who made a mistake, a mistake covered by hiding and adoption. In other words, it was a traditional maternity home. Staff members, particularly those who had been with Hawthorne House for some time and were responsible for putting into practice newer and more professional conceptions of unwed mothers, thus saw their newer policies and practices in contrast to what had gone before.

So, for example, *responsibility* had a particular meaning for the staff in being posed against what was felt to be the overprotectiveness of the House in the past.

> Mrs. Fleischmann said, "I think it is very much our philosophy now. I think if there was one word to be written over the door as you entered, that would be it—responsibility. And it is very much a change from the way the home used to be. It used to be incredibly overprotective. For example, people who ran the home years ago used to feel sheepish about even presenting the girl a bill when she left. They would hand her a little slip of paper and suggest that maybe she might think about this amount. And in many cases, a bill was never even mentioned. I think this is a service and it should be paid for, and that this is part of the responsibility thing. It used to be run much more like a charity and was very overprotective of the girls. You know, we had a whole system of addresses that were fictitious and girls used to get mail through them. [Her tone was disapproving.]
>
> "After all, girls come here because they acted irresponsibly to start with, particularly now that ways to prevent getting pregnant are so common. And I don't think we should encourage that kind of thing. A lot of what we try to do is based on this philosophy that girls should be

encouraged to accept responsibility for themselves, and to take responsibility."

The staff critically examined a number of practices common to maternity homes, and up until recently characteristic of Hawthorne House, in the light of their conceptions of responsibility, denial, and the sources of illegitimate pregnancy. For example, in the service of secrecy, it is customary for girls in maternity homes to avoid using their last names (some girls even use alias first names), to develop a *story*— frequently a medical story—to explain their lengthy absence from school or home, and to *cover* their situation in public by wearing phony wedding rings and by answering casual questions with purposely vague or uncheckable information about nonexistent husbands or households. Maternity homes have traditionally supported these evasions through such institutional practices as avoiding the use of last names (which means, for example, guarded and careful distribution of the mail) and the provision of phony addresses and phony medical records. Even more fundamentally, maternity homes have traditionally supported girls' intentions for adoption by making special arrangements with hospitals so that girls who wish it need never see their babies.[6]

It was in contrast to these common practices, therefore, that the staff at Hawthorne House developed and expressed their own understandings of responsibility and denial.

Mrs. Richter raised the question of the use of the girls' last names, saying she was confused about whether last names were to be used or not. Mrs. Fleischmann had an immediate reaction to this, "Well, we put in a lot of staff

6. For example, in a published account of the diary she kept while becoming an unwed mother in a Salvation Army home in the early 1960's, "Jean Thompson" reports her use of a fictional name and hometown, the general nonuse of last names, and the option to be blindfolded during delivery. (Thompson, 1967)

time about six or nine months ago in working out this decision, and there are very good reasons for it—things having to do with facing reality and accepting the fact of pregnancy. We decided at that time that all girls were to use their last names, and that the staff should use the girls' last names. The only exceptions are in the newspaper which goes out to the public and on the board by the switchboard (near the public entrance) for the same reason. But we do want last names used."

A group of older girls, who worked during the day and who lived together in a separate residence under the auspices of Hawthorne House, prepared a booklet which they felt would be helpful for other future girls who planned to work while pregnant. The booklet was discussed in staff meeting during which objections were raised to the following section.

WORKING FOR MANPOWER
. . . Another helpful suggestion is to purchase a wedding band of some type to help avoid many questions. . . . You should be prepared to answer questions such as: your maiden name, husband's first, husband's job or school, preferably not the service, and/or how long you have been in the city. After working on the job for some time, be prepared for such things as: your boss asking you to change for a permanent position from the Manpower agency, or the women may decide to give you a baby shower, or employees may ask to give you a ride home.

The most helpful hint we can offer if you find yourself employed by Manpower is to make sure you have your "story" straight. Of course it is up to the individual what the "story" will be, but if you can remember to plan ahead, you will not have to experience any type of embarrassment while working. In planning your "story" make sure it is as close to a real situation as possible: names, places, etc.

With reference to this section, Mrs. Rhodes objected: "Furthermore, this business about rings and stories—I don't know if it's a good idea to contribute to that sort of thing in the booklet. I don't know if that goes along with our philosophy or not. I don't think we should help people out with their denial. I think there are a lot of issues raised by the booklet that should be discussed before we pass it out."

Perhaps the most important of these psychiatrically understood issues had to do with the relationship between girls and their babies. For a large part of accepting and not denying pregnancy, from the staff's point of view, had to do with accepting the baby. In a variety of ways, the staff were psychiatrically concerned that girls experience maximal involvement in becoming and being mothers, both during pregnancy and during and following delivery. So, for example, the staff spoke favorably of methods of delivery which allowed girls to be awake and aware of birth.

As the most important and systematic of these policies, the Hawthorne House staff strongly urged girls both to see and to feed their babies in the hospital—in other words, to act toward their babies as mothers normally would following delivery. This policy, and its psychological rationale, are reflected in the following excerpt from the clinical psychologist's account of a group-therapy meeting.

> Early in the meeting Jeanne took a position very similar to that of Avis in prior meetings, that is . . . she did not intend to feed her baby and that she strongly resented what she felt as powerful pressures being placed on her by the staff at the Home to see her baby. What right did they have, she asked, to try and tell her what is best for her. The main part of the meeting was devoted to an effort on the part of Marlene and Laura to convince Jeanne that she ought to see her baby and that her way of dealing with the problem was one of denying reality.
>
> Leader attempted to play a fairly neutral part in this discussion but to open up to inquiry Jeanne's reasons for setting

herself against the combined opinions of everyone in her environment. It was in this context that Jeanne was able to verbalize that her fear was of becoming so attached to the baby that she couldn't give it up and that meant she had to cut herself off from any sort of tie with it.

In a number of ways, therefore, the staff at Hawthorne House were led by their professional and psychiatric conceptions of illegitimate pregnancy and unwed mothers to question practices which have been typical of maternity homes and to understand and deal with their clients in newer ways. Yet Hawthorne House was nevertheless a maternity home, recruiting clients for traditional services—secrecy and adoption; this fact was both a problem and a point of leverage for the staff in implementing their conceptions.

SECRECY

While concerned that excessive preoccupation with the mechanics of secrecy allowed girls to deny their situation, the Hawthorne House staff were also aware that secrecy was their clients' first concern, as well as one of Hawthorne House's central reasons for existence. And, in fact, a number of routines in the home were shaped by the requirements of secrecy. Last names were not used or listed in circumstances which might reach beyond the House, girls were instructed not to use the name of the House in answering the phone, and the names of visitors to the House were posted in advance so that girls might remain upstairs to avoid being seen by someone they knew or by someone from their home town.

In other ways as well, and in spite of their reservations, the staff had to recognize the necessity of some strategies for maintaining discretion in the outside world.

Continuing her discussion of intake procedures for the staff, Mrs. Fleischmann said, "Now, one of the issues that will come up, and which really presents a problem for our philosophy and for the home, is the question of cover stories. We do not tell a family what cover story to use, although we may suggest ones that other families have used. We mostly tell them that the story, whatever it is, should be consistent. They shouldn't tell Aunt Sarah one thing and Uncle So-and-So something else because they're sure to get together and compare notes. The story should be consistent and told that way to everyone. The home as such, however, does not provide alibis or false addresses and such. We used to at one time. We also don't provide phony medical reasons. If they can get their hometown doctor to certify that they've had mononucleosis, well, that's one thing, but I don't know if there are many ethical doctors that would do so."

To some extent, therefore, the staff regarded formal secrecy practices as a concession to the concerns of their clients, a concession which was a problem for House philosophy. Yet it was also true that the staff did not regard secrecy simply as an unavoidable and distasteful necessity, but as one of the appropriate uses to make of Hawthorne House.

During the tea following medical clinic, Mrs. Fleischmann came in and got some tea from Sally. She said to Sally, "Are you going to the beach party? Oh, I guess you're not because it is so close to home."

Sally replied, "Oh, I'm going; all my friends at home know anyway. I see them when I go home to visit anyway."

A little later, Mrs. Fleischmann and I were talking at some distance from Sally; she said, shaking her head over Sally, "When I think of all the people that we could use our facilities to be helping—people who really care whether other people know—it just kills me to think that these kids don't make use of it. There are a couple around like that."

The staff expected girls to enter the House with a keen sense of their situation, as well as with the conventional set of reasons for coming to a maternity home. There was, therefore, a sense in which the staff could afford to abandon an official concern with secrecy because their clients could generally be counted on to improvise their own secrecy practices. It is interesting to note, for example, that in spite of House policy, girls did not use last names during the time I spent at Hawthorne House and referred to each other by first name and last initial.

Girls who were unconcerned with secrecy, girls who were not upset by their situation, and girls who were not in some way asking for help presented problems for the staff not only in being psychiatrically unavailable but also in not acting the way girls in trouble would naturally act—in fact, ought to act.

During informal discussion at staff coffee a couple of girls' names came up. Mrs. Hilton said about Jeanne, "She's just impossible. She's a really way-out kid. She comes in and says, 'I don't need any counseling, I don't want any counseling. If I should want counseling, I can talk to my parents or minister.'"

Mrs. Hilton continued, "She also says that the only reason she got pregnant is because she had an apartment alone when she was at college. She is twenty-two years old and a graduate student and she can say something like that. Boy, if we only accepted those who were suitable for treatment, she wouldn't be here."

❀　❀　❀

I remarked to Mrs. Collins how expressive Emily had been in the new girls' meeting. Mrs. Collins said, "Well, the staff is fairly upset with her—perhaps you noticed. Apparently she caused a lot of trouble in looking at a large number of maternity homes. She would come here and say that another maternity home didn't have such-and-such and then she would go there and say things about Hawthorne House. But that business of comparing the different agencies to each other got the staff upset. And then she came in yesterday. She was supposed to come in the morning and she didn't show up until 2 in the afternoon; then the minute she got in, she expected to be seen by somebody. This, of course, upset the staff too. I think they felt she was manipulating them."

❋ ❋ ❋

During casual conversation among the staff about various girls, Mrs. Fleischmann said of Debbie, "She's always so rosy, as if nothing was happening at all. It's just impossible to work with her."

While the staff thus preferred to take a psychiatric view toward their clients, this view was grounded on a set of more practical expectations as to how unwed mothers usually and normally feel and act—namely, that unwed mothers can usually be relied on to take their situation very seriously.

I have already suggested that maternity homes have traditionally supported a view of their clients as essentially *good girls* who made a mistake. By contrast, Hawthorne House was not officially concerned with its clients' moral status nor with the reinstatement of respectability. Yet, less officially, the staff relied on the girls' own sense of jeopardized moral status not only as a way of involving them in the therapeutic rationale of the House but also as a way of enforcing some notions of respectability in the House.

RESPECTABILITY

The rules and expectations which governed daily life in the House were much like those usually in force for girls in other settings—college dormitories and at home—and covered such matters as appropriate dress in the public areas of the House, hours, and signing out procedures. Unlike the inmates of some other kinds of institutions for deviants, the girls at Hawthorne House did not encounter rules which expressed a specific regard for the shameful aspects of their situation,[7] nor did they confront the more general assaults on identity which Erving Goffman (1961) has described for larger or more disciplinary "total institutions."[8]

In this sense, the rules at Hawthorne House had no special relevance to the girls' current situations, except for the very important implication that such rules were still in moral force and were not invalidated or made less necessary by the girls' unrespectable situation. In fact, the special significance of these rules for girls at Hawthorne House can best be expressed in the sentiment that, "Now that this has happened, and especially while you are *in* this situation, you have to be *all the more careful*."

In defense of the rules, as well as in less prescribed encounters with girls over matters of appropriate dress, manner, and behavior, the staff expressed their views of the ladylike behavior ordinarily expected of girls, and all the more necessary for girls who are illegitimately pregnant.

The nurse, Mrs. Van Riper, was running an informal discussion in the girls' lounge as a part of the prenatal

7. Some rules were specifically designed to the girls' situation, but these were medically justified rules—for example, girls were required to be in bed by 10 p.m., except for two nights a week when they could stay up until 11 p.m.

8. Girls were not, for example, issued standard institutional dress but could wear their own clothes or pick from a stock of maternity clothes kept in the House. These institutionally provided garments belonged to a girl until she returned them or "willed" them to another girl. Because girls also treated their own maternity clothes this way, frequently leaving them to the House by way of a friend, dress had the opposite consequence usual to total institutions, serving primarily as a way of shedding a disinherited identity upon leaving.

series, "There have been girls in the hospital who don't seem to have any sense of how to conduct themselves. They walk down the corridors in bare feet and half-exposed and don't seem to care what the other married women think of their conduct or the impression they are making. I think it is a matter of modesty and that it is related to how you would feel about yourself outside. If you act that way after you get out of the hospital, outside, you will find yourself in trouble. You have to have a certain respect for yourself and how you appear to other people. I think, for example, a girl should not lie around half-exposed when she is having male visitors. This gives a very bad impression to other people."

❋   ❋   ❋

In a meeting of all girls new to the House, Dale asked, "Well, I was wondering about another rule. I was wondering, is it true that we can't wear shorts downstairs or outside the home?"

Mrs. Collins stated the rule which is that you can wear shorts only upstairs in the House.

Dale said, "I just don't understand that. I think shorts look very trim and cute on a lot of kids. They look better than these baggy, old smocks, and if you're sitting around it just looks much better than having to worry how you're sitting. You can sit any way you want. I just don't understand the reason for this rule. I can see maybe when you have visitors in the home, they might prefer you to wear dresses and look more ladylike. But. . . ."

Mrs. Collins interrupted, "Why not with visitors?"

Dale said, "Well, it's just more ladylike if you have a dress on." Mrs. Collins kept pressing her on this and was obviously trying to get Dale to defend the rule inadvertently. Dale again protested the rule, and Mrs. Collins said, "Well, this comes up all the time and particularly in the summer. We feel it's all right upstairs in the House, and when you go outside for barbecues. But otherwise, if you're downstairs, there are likely to be girls and their parents who are coming in for their first interview, or visitors, and there's no way girls can avoid the living room. We just feel it looks nicer, and, as you say, there may be some girls who look bad in shorts and how are we going to tell one girl she can't wear them?"

She later added, "You have to remember that we also live in a community, and that they may feel strongly about girls wearing shorts, particularly when they're pregnant."

Emily added, "You'd be surprised at how many people there are who feel strongly about pregnant women wearing shorts, period, let alone if they're unmarried."

Someone else said, "I know that was true in my college too. There was a beach across from the college, and we were not allowed to come back across the street wearing bathing suits or carrying an open can of beer. We always had to be wearing skirts." There was a lot of agreement about this, and the subject passed.

Because the staff could rely on girls' past training in matters of respectable appearance, as well as on the girls' own sense of the special requirements of their current situation, dramatic violations of the canons of respectability rarely came up for overt and concerted response on the part of the staff. Instead, respectability was an underlying theme in the House, generally taken for granted and arising for discussion only around relatively mild refinements of good taste.

Yet the handling of mild issues of respectability can be used to illustrate an important aspect of the girls' experience at Hawthorne House. Matters of respectability, like other more serious matters, were usually handled individually as part of the relationship between the girl and her caseworker.

The following, more publicly discussed episode, suggests that the staff relied, in their handling of such matters, on the girls' own sense of ambivalent moral status to direct them to decisions. By this, I do not mean that the staff used a stance of therapeutic neutrality to engineer consent to decisions favored by the staff. Because the girls felt a particular vulnerability to questions of good taste and respectability, they were inclined, when left to the dictates of conscience, to make the most morally conservative decision. And, in some areas, girls made decisions which in fact countered staff opinion.[9]

Yet the practice of a kind of neutrality gave to the girls' experiences in the House a quality which heightened a sense of ambivalent moral status, and balanced this against protection from stigma and an eventual sense of moral reprieve.

During a meeting of girls who were officers of the House with some staff members, Peg asked, "Can I bring up the subject of my dress?" She then explained, "Well, I have this dress, and it has bloomers, and Mrs. Bishop [a member of the House staff who runs the switchboard] yelled at me the other day about wearing it. I guess I could understand if it were real short, but it's not that much shorter than the dresses a lot of girls around here wear. But she yelled at me for it, and I was wondering if I should wear it again, or if I would get yelled at."

No one seemed to know how to react at first, and their way of reacting was to ask more about the dress.

Peg continued, "It's just a plain dress. It's sort of beige; it doesn't stand out in any particular way. It's not flashy or

9. The girls' feelings regarding contraceptive preparation, for example, expressed a more conservative view of their sexual future than many staff members felt was either accurate or necessary. This issue is described more fully in Chapter 4.

anything . . . it has pantaloons which stick out a little bit underneath it. I guess it was the pantaloons that made her say that, but I can't see what's so wrong with it."

Mrs. Wilson said, "Well, Mrs. Lewin and I saw a girl the other day that had bloomers on with a dress, and it looked very modest. We thought it was quite cute. . . ." It was obvious no one knew what to say.

Mrs. Lewin said, after a bit of silence, "We don't have any specific rules about how short dresses can be around here. I think we try to stress that girls should dress so as not to call attention to themselves. In part, this is a function of our relationships with our neighbors. We try to antagonize them as little as possible, and in return we wish they wouldn't antagonize us so much."

At one point, it was suggested that Peg go put on the dress, which she did. She returned and everybody said, "Oh, that's cute," and things like that. It was about three or four inches above the knees and had pants underneath that had a lace edge which showed beneath the dress.

Mrs. Lewin said, "Well, I can kind of see that the pants are additional. Maybe that's what Mrs. Bishop objected to." At another point, she said, "Well, you know how Mrs. Bishop is. Sometimes the way she says things isn't what she really means."

Peg said, "Well, I just wanted to know if I could wear it again or whether I'd get yelled at." At several points during the discussion she was on the verge of tears, and she kept saying things like, "It really bothered me because I don't try to look flashy or call attention to myself, or any of those things, and then I got yelled at and I felt cheap and everything."

The question seemed to be left up in the air. After a more general discussion of rules for dress, Mrs. Lewin said, "Well, I think the thing to keep in mind is that all girls should dress so as not to call attention to themselves, and to dress in a modest fashion, particularly given their condition. You have to be all the more careful. It is easy to have the way you dress be misinterpreted by other people, and I think in this situation, we're all interested in not calling attention to ourselves."

One of the advantages of entering a maternity home, recognized by both staff and girls, is that it frees the girl from having to present herself as normal and happy to those who don't know her situation and from having to present herself as continuously upset to those who do know. Nevertheless, even within the House where girls are more free to express their own moods of happiness and sadness, the expectation that girls are to take their situation seriously sets limits on their behavior and serves as a constant background reminder that their situation is serious.

Mrs. Morgan raised the question of girls hanging around the downstairs living room, "I've noticed there are a number of girls who just hang out in the living room all day. They don't do anything, and they're not waiting for anyone. They just hang around to see what's going on and to look over the new girls. I was wondering if this was a very good idea or if there's some way we could get them out of there."

Mrs. Jasperson said, "I think it gives a very bad impression to the new girls that are coming in with their parents. They sit around and they're very upset, and there are these girls kind of sitting around, and laughing and joking."

The girls themselves are aware, in the midst of their happier moments, of the constant possibility that they will be called upon to become serious and that they will, in fact, *be* recalled to their more serious feelings.

During group-therapy meeting there was a lot of silence. Lillian said, "I don't know about other people, but I just feel content. I just walked down the hill, and maybe it was my high bowling score, or I don't know what, but I just feel content. Maybe I won't feel this way later, and maybe later I'll be sobbing and crying and everything, but right now I just feel happy and content. And I don't feel much like saying anything."

BECOMING A MOTHER

The issue of greatest moral and psychiatric salience in the House had to do with the relationship of the girls to their babies. The staff were concerned that the girls go through the experience of becoming a mother in as positive, normal, and natural a way as possible. Psychiatrically, as I have said, the staff were concerned with the experience of becoming a mother in terms of the issue of denial, an issue related to staff conceptions of the causes of illegitimate pregnancy, and the treatment of unwed mothers.

This view was supported, however, by the more fundamental and moral conviction that becoming a mother was the girls' main concern during their stay at Hawthorne House, and that any woman facing one of life's most momentous occasions will normally and naturally have strong feelings for her baby and a motherly concern for her baby's welfare. The staff's concern for *normalizing* the girls' experience of becoming a mother, expressed for example in the opinion that girls should see and feed their babies, backed a psychiatric rationale with a view of what is natural and right for mothers to feel.

The part Hawthorne House played in shaping the girls' experience of becoming a mother cannot be overemphasized. First, girls who came to the home did not necessarily and naturally feel upon entering the House that becoming a mother was the central feature of their experience in being pregnant out of wedlock. Many girls, for example, were initially much more concerned with their newly conflicted relationships with boyfriends or parents than with becoming a mother. While most girls shifted their central attention to the baby under the combined effect of progressing pregnancy and House opinion, some did not and experienced comment of both a moral and psychiatric kind.

In a group-therapy meeting Avis said, "I had something I wanted to bring up. I was wondering what you all felt the relationship between your feelings toward the father and your feelings toward the baby are. I mean, I was wondering if they are related—if they seem that way to you?"

Shirley said, "I think they're separate feelings for me. I'm angry at the father, but I'm not toward the baby. You can't take it out on the baby."

Several girls agreed, and Dr. Hildreth commented, "You feel more like a twosome than a threesome."

Mary Ann said, "That's really hard for me to understand—how they can be such separate feelings. I can't imagine what it would feel like to bear a baby of someone that you not only didn't love, but didn't even like."

Dr. Hildreth said, "You feel more like a threesome than a twosome."

Avis said, "I was thinking that it's hard to separate the two feelings, but I guess it isn't."

Laura said, mostly to Avis, "Well, here, I'll give you something different. I know several girls that I've talked to in the House that are just waiting to get married after this is over. They view the baby as an inconvenience to be gotten out of the way."

Avis was amazed and said, "Really. I find that so hard to believe."

Laura said, disapprovingly, "It's a twosome, but the baby is the outsider for them."

Glenda then said, "I can't understand why anyone who is going with a fellow all during pregnancy and plans to marry him would give up the baby." She sounded amazed.

Shirley, also disbelieving, said, "I've heard that, too."

Laura said, "I don't know. Perhaps because they're younger, their families say 'yes,' but are really hoping that they won't get married and will break up afterwards." She gave this explanation for their motives, but looked sympathetic to the people who were objecting.

Then Susan said, "Well, I am still in love with and going with the father of my child, and he wants to marry me, and I probably will. But I want to wait a year because I don't want to jump into things without being sure." I think someone asked if she was giving up the baby and she said, "Yes."

Dr. Hildreth said, "Do you really think you could marry a man by whom you have had a child that you have given up?" Susan nodded, and he said again, "Do you really think that is possible?" It was quite clear from his tone that he did not think it was.

Second, while girls generally shared the view that a mother would naturally have certain feelings for her child, the way in which these feelings ought to be linked to actual decisions about the baby was by no means apparent. One of the most difficult features for girls in making decisions about their babies was the fact that the arguments made *both for and against* any line of action were expressed in terms of a mother's natural feelings for her baby, and her motherly concern for her baby's welfare.

So, for example, the sentiment *How can you give up your own child?* and the sentiment that a girl would be selfish and unmotherly to sacrifice her baby's welfare and stable future by keeping an illegitimate child in a one-parent situation are both based on the same premise that a mother loves and cares for her child.

Similarly, the same premise may justify opposite decisions about seeing the baby.

Marlene talked to me about Jeanne's defense in a group meeting of her decision not to see or feed her baby, "We all kept telling her what a wonderful experience it is, and how much she is missing, but she just kept saying, 'I know, I know. That's why I don't think I could give up the baby after doing it.'"

Many girls came to the House advised by others *not* to become involved with their babies lest the pain of separation be unnecessarily great and lest the decision for adoption be jeopardized. Because girls do become involved with their babies regardless of any intention not to, the Hawthorne House orientation was persuasive not only because it provided a clear and strongly put psychiatric rationale for one line of action but also because it recommended that girls act as mothers naturally would act. And most girls in the House did see and feed their babies in spite of their entering intention not to.

The group-therapy discussion turned to seeing and feeding the baby. Several girls mentioned advice they had gotten on this subject before they had come to the home. Shirley said, "My doctor who sent me here urged me not to see the baby. He said it would only make it harder."

Glenda said, "I know my parents didn't want me to see the baby."

Kim said, "My mother didn't want me to see the baby, and, in fact, I was planning not to."

Earlier in the discussion, Avis had reacted to Laura's comments about painful realization working against denial. Avis said, "I sometimes wonder why you should want to increase the amount of pain you feel. I mean, you don't ordinarily seek out painful experiences in other areas of life. Why should you in this one?" Now she added, "I can sort of see the point. I know I wasn't going to see the baby at first, but I took my social worker's word that it was the best thing to do. I figured she'd seen more girls and probably knew better."

While staff expectations, in their view, served to uncover already existing feelings and to allow girls to express their natural feelings, it is also true that the staff expectations in some measure served to create feelings appropriate to a mother normally.

Becoming an unwed mother, particularly one who intends to give up her child, is after all different in some crucial aspects from becoming a mother in more usual circumstances, and some feelings normal to mothers will be accentuated, while other feelings will be absent. For example, unwed mothers are likely to feel more exclusively responsible for their babies' eventual welfare, on the one hand, and yet, on the other hand, this responsibility is somewhat abstract, for girls who give up their babies do not become involved in actually caring for their babies' immediate needs.

Even within the framework of the staff's concern for *normalizing* the experience of becoming a mother there were problems, problems which centered around the adoption decision. Adoption raised questions not easily encompassed by understandings of a mother's normal and natural feelings and responsibilities.

ADOPTION DECISIONS

Girls who planned to place their babies for adoption, and most girls at Hawthorne House did, had to draw lines and make decisions with which a *normal* mother is not faced. So, for example, a girl may determine, or hope to determine, some aspects of her baby's future, but not others. Girls could specify the religion of the adoptive parents and could hope through discussions with the adoption agency worker to have other preferences taken into account; girls could not, of course, meet the prospective parents, nor could they name their babies, except temporarily.

The actual responsibility a girl may take for her baby's future may fit neither her own conceptions of responsible action nor even legal conceptions of legitimate responsibility. Furthermore, a girl may question what right she has, once she has decided to give up her child, to even these relatively meager decisions.

Laura, an ex-Catholic, said, "I myself am an atheist, but that is a conviction I arrived at by choice. But I wanted to pick a religion for my baby so that he could grow up with some background in religion and also make a choice. I am very interested in religion and I've thought a lot about it. I said I wanted my baby to go into a Jewish home, because I figured that was a very rational religion and that this would give my baby a background from which he could choose later. . . . Also . . . I understood that there are very few babies specifically to be placed in Jewish homes, so the demand is very high, and I thought this increased the chances of getting the kind of home that I wanted."

Avis asked at one point, "What happens if you don't sign the religious waiver?"

Laura said, "The baby then goes to a home of the same religion as the mother by law. It's her choice."

Avis said, "It seems funny to me. I mean if you've made the decision about giving the baby up, really what right do you have to make these kinds of decisions? It just seems funny." She sounded very reflective, but no one took up what she said except Laura who made one comment, "I have questioned that myself. Why is that particular decision so important?"

In addition to the question of the areas of responsibility a girl may take for the child she is giving up, there is also a question as to when a girl is and is no longer a mother and, as such, responsible for her child. While the following case was an exceptional one, it is nevertheless true that at some point a girl who gives up her baby must abandon her motherly concern for her child, and this point does not necessarily coincide with the signing of legal papers.

Mrs. Hilton responded to another caseworker, "Well, I know the case that's most recently on our minds. A girl with a sick baby. I was really quite shocked that she signed the surrender papers and left for home when the baby was still over in the hospital. I think that raises the real question of the girl's responsibility for the baby—even if the agency is willing to take the surrender."

For both the girls and staff at Hawthorne House, decisions like these were less easily fitted to conceptions of normal motherly feelings and responsibilities than the decision about seeing and feeding the baby. The most serious problems were, however, raised by the issue of adoption itself. Briefly, the staff emphasis on normalizing the experience of becoming a mother tended to make an open issue of adoption in a setting in which adoption was, nevertheless, virtually a foregone conclusion.

ADOPTION

The staff at Hawthorne House, unlike that at many maternity homes, preferred to think of adoptive placement as an open issue rather than as a foregone conclusion. In part, this preference was congruent with their emphasis, as professionally trained caseworkers, on the importance of dealing with clients on an individual, and not a pre-determined basis. And in large part, this preference had to do with their psychologically based concern with the possible deep and long-term effects on a girl of giving up her child.

Someone at the lunch table made a comment about the conference Lois was going to be in today. I said, "What is that?"

Lois said, "Oh, they're going to have this big thing with my mother and father and Mrs. Morgan and Dr. Balfour and me. It's going to be a giant conference. I just hope I don't cry all the time, as usual. She sort of wants me to plan on getting married, I think, and I keep telling her I'm not ready to. I guess that's what we're going to talk about."

Julie said, "I don't think they should pressure you so much."

Lois said, "Well, it's not that exactly. I just guess Mrs. Morgan thinks that when I see the baby, I'll wish I had decided to get married. She thinks that later I may regret not having gotten married."

The staff regarded adoption as a very serious and difficult decision which ought not to be made lightly or automatically —*in either direction*—and which ought to be examined in the light of every alternative, as well as the possible ramifications. Because most girls entered the home with the intention to have their babies adopted, staff concern tended to take the form of encouraging girls to examine the alternatives to adoption.

At some point during group-therapy discussion, Marlene, who had delivered, made a comment to the effect that it wasn't so easy to give up a child once you had it as you might think. Lillian said, "I know that. Don't you think I haven't thought about keeping him myself. I even explored the possibility of working as a housekeeper. I called the man and everything. It's not a matter of money. I know my parents are very well off, and they certainly would support me, so it's not really that. . . . I just keep thinking is that the best thing. I mean what are you going to say, how are you going to explain it to a child when he gets a little older?"

Dr. Hildreth said, "Explain what?"

Lillian said, "That his father isn't around. And can you give a child all the advantages of being in a family when he's not really in a family?"

Millie added, "And you wouldn't be able to really give him the advantages of a family. You'd always have the problem of the name and being illegitimate."

Marlene broke in to say, "Well, I can give you one exception to what you're talking about. I know I'm in the situation you were talking about and I went to college for two years, and I've made out all right. My mother had me out of wedlock. I'm illegitimate and so are my brothers and sisters and we've done all right. . . . I just thought I'd say that so you'd keep it in mind that it isn't impossible. There is an exception sitting right here."

Lillian looked at Marlene in absolute amazement, "I'm stunned. I absolutely don't know what to say. I'm just stunned."

Marlene was equally surprised by Lillian's reaction, and started to get annoyed and defensive.

At several points during this discussion, Dr. Hildreth mentioned having real alternatives—that is, considering all the alternatives, really considering them. After Marlene's statement, Dr. Hildreth said toward Lillian, "Now you have an alternative." At a later point when Lillian insisted she had considered the alternatives, he said, "But they weren't *real* alternatives."

Yet the staff were also concerned with the decision of girls who planned to keep their babies. For while adoption raised staff concern for the mothers who were giving up their babies, keeping the baby raised staff concern about the baby's future welfare. First, the staff, familiar with and oriented to a girl's psychological problems and her progress in understanding these problems, were likely to forecast her mothering abilities in the light of their observations.

During the psychiatric staff meeting, Dr. Balfour mentioned Marlene's decision after delivery to keep her baby. Several case workers looked fairly negative about this. Mrs. Hilton said, "That poor baby. Wait till it starts to walk. I just feel sorry for the baby, that's all." Others mirrored the same feeling.

Second, the staff were likely to view a girl's decision to keep her baby not only in terms of the realistic conditions for supporting and caring for a child, but also in terms of psychologically oriented conceptions of ideal conditions for raising a child. The staff, for example, had real reservations about the welfare of a child raised in a one-parent home and were much more likely to favor keeping the baby for girls who could choose to marry the father of their child. These reservations can best be expressed in the words of one caseworker during a discussion of an outside research worker's observations that, while not ideal, there were an increasing number of viable one-parent homes, and that maternity homes might consider recommending that more girls keep their babies.

"You know, you talk about the one-parent family becoming a more common social entity. But I wonder sometimes how much we can support a social change like that before we see its effect. Maybe I'm too much involved in the old way things have been organized in the social system. But I can't help but think diagnostically that a one-parent family is going to have bad effects on the children that are raised in it. I mean, nobody knows the real effect of that kind of system on the children, and I can't see myself recommending it."

Because in fact most girls were likely to place their babies for adoption, and because the staff in many if not most cases were likely to feel that this was the most reasonable alternative, the emphasis on making the experience of becoming a mother as normal as possible raised problems for the girls and for the staff—because to act as a mother normally does may well place the question of adoption in jeopardy.

During a group-therapy meeting, Avis mentioned that her social worker had recommended that she see the baby but not feed it. Dr. Hildreth asked, "Why do you think she said this to you?"

Avis thought for a minute or so, and said, reflectively, "I really don't know."

Kim said, "Mine said the same thing to me too."

Dr. Hildreth asked, "Who is your social worker?"

Kim said, "Mrs. Fleischmann." This was also Avis' social worker. There was then a brief discussion in which Dr. Hildreth found out that other girls had Mrs. Fleischmann but had not necessarily received the same advice. He asked Kim, "Why do you think she recommended this for you?"

Kim said, "Well, I think it had something to do with my mother talking to her. I only heard when I was in the wage home that it was the policy here to see the baby. I didn't want to see the baby and neither did my mother want me to. I think she probably spoke to Mrs. Fleischmann and said how hard it would be if I did." Several girls objected that they couldn't imagine Mrs. Fleischmann backing down or changing her mind just because of pressure from parents.

Dr. Hildreth asked Avis again why she thought she had received the advice she had. Avis said, "I think maybe she's afraid that if I do too much, I will change my mind about adoption."

Kim added, "And that's one thing she in particular doesn't want, not for anyone. I don't think she thinks any girl here is capable of raising a child." There was a long silence after this.

Whatever special temperings of House philosophy were made to fit the particular situations of particular girls, the House orientation to adoption must be understood in terms of their view of adoption as a serious and difficult decision. For the general effect of staff concerns to allow and encourage normal motherly feelings was to balance the girls' strong feelings for their babies against their original intentions in coming to a maternity home, and thereby to make adoption a serious and difficult decision indeed.

Visiting Jerri in the hospital during her last days there, I asked, "And has your social worker come to visit like you were joking about that day?"

Jerri said, "Oh yes. She's trying to get me to keep the baby. She keeps telling me, 'Don't make up your mind too harshly.'"

I said, "That surprises me. I thought that by and large social workers advise girls to have their babies adopted."

She said, "I guess in my case it's because I'm still going with the boy. She keeps saying not to make up my mind too harshly. But I don't know how I could support the baby. And then all the people at home would know. I mean it seems kind of silly to pay all this money to go away. That's what most girls go away for—and then to come home with the baby. And what would I do? I have no way of supporting it and taking care of it at the same time. I mean maybe my mother could take care of it, but I don't know. She's been going with this guy lately, and he doesn't know anything about it. He's sort of straitlaced, and if he found out about it, he'd be really upset—also because she hasn't told him. But she wants me to keep the baby too. I just can't see it. I'd really like to, but I don't know how I could do it."

Jerri looked torn up by her considerations. She had been crying and was on the verge of tears.

SUMMARY

Unlike traditional maternity homes, Hawthorne House was not officially concerned with respectability and moral reinstatement, but with the psychological dimensions of their clients' experiences. On the one hand, the staff were concerned with the psychological sources, the problems, manifested in an illegitimate pregnancy, but, on the other hand, they were concerned with the normal features of becoming a mother.

Like most maternity homes, however, Hawthorne House recruited self-selected volunteers with a special sense of their situation and a special set of reasons for being there. These reasons may be termed *respectability concerns.* In this sense, while committed to newer conceptions of its function, Hawthorne House nevertheless also served the traditional purposes of maternity homes. On the one hand, the official House orientations snagged at the points where these orientations ran up against the usual purposes of maternity homes—specifically, over secrecy practices and adoption. Yet on the other hand, the traditional features and interests of their clients served as the taken-for-granted background for the working of official concerns.

4

The Moral Career
of the Unwed Mother

Motherhood is still the supreme state for a woman and the conditions under which it was brought about may be ignored after the child is a fait accompli. . . . The unwed mother, although violating some moral standards, has fulfilled important American values and may be less condemned than tolerated, and more accepted than understood. . . .

The white subculture officially views illegitimacy with shock; . . . The white girl tries to find some good that can be interpreted as resulting from her transgression to make it appear less serious. The white girl therefore is likely to say she has "learned her lesson." She has probably been encouraged to look within herself for the reasons for her mistake because white subculture stresses individual responsibility for error.

Bowerman, Irish, and Pope
(1963–1966: 320–321, 329)

The moral career of a girl who becomes an unwed mother at Hawthorne House begins, upon entrance, with the experience of moral rescue—an experience shaped particularly by the characteristics Hawthorne House shares with most maternity homes. As she spends time there, however, she encounters the directly and systematically expressed House view of what she is doing there. While I have drawn on girls'

89

experiences at Hawthorne House as a way of developing a description of staff orientations, I have not directly described what girls made of their encounter with the House.

It is the task of this chapter then to describe how girls understood the orientations of the House, particularly what girls came to believe about themselves and their situation as a result of their encounter with Hawthorne House. The crucial features of this encounter include conversion to a psychiatric version of the past—a conversion with somewhat paradoxical implications for future sexual behavior, an institutional experience closely geared to the passage of time and to progress toward the predicted due date, and a gradual shift from respectability to motherhood as the central issue defining the girls' situation.

CONVERSION TO A PSYCHIATRIC VERSION OF THE PAST

While perhaps not a seriously or deeply as the staff might have wished, most girls in the House did come to an agreement with the psychiatric view of their situation. There were some girls, particularly the younger ones less given to self-analysis and self-reflective group discussion, who managed to ignore a psychological interpretation of illegitimate pregnancy and to retain a view of their situation as a mistake. And there were a few girls who more actively challenged and successfully resisted the House orientation. Yet for most girls, conversion to a psychiatric version of their situation was a central feature of their initial experience at Hawthorne House, forming a second stage in their careers through the House.

While the House psychiatric orientation was systematically formulated and expressed in the ways I have already described, two features particularly enhanced its effectiveness with the girls. First, unlike the psychiatric or treatment orientations of other sorts of institutions with a more diverse set of inmates, the same interpretive scheme was roughly applicable to everyone. For although the staff emphasized the importance of individual and individualized casework, their professional understandings of illegitimate pregnancy and their routine experience with unwed mothers made the range of interpretation a good deal narrower and more specific than would, for example, be possible in a mental hospital or juvenile institution. Furthermore, in order to convey even a general psychiatric orientation to their clients, the staff had to speak more simplistically, more dogmatically, than they might have wished.

The effect of an interpretive scheme roughly applicable to everyone was that the girls themselves could and did serve as interpreters of the House-sponsored view of unwed mothers to each other in their numerous, often serious, everyday discussions. In this way, conversion to a psychiatric version of their stiuation was expressed, indeed enforced, by the girls themselves, particularly in conversation with newcomers to the House.

The second feature of the psychiatric version of their situation which the girls found particularly persuasive was the implied, sometimes stated, threat of a second illegitimate pregnancy at some point in the future. For the staff, the view that psychological problems and patterns of behavior do not simply cease with a dramatic and troublesome event but reoccur unless some understanding or resolution is reached was an expression of an accepted and very general psychiatric principle. In this sense, the staff view of the future was less a deliberate and specific threat than a somewhat incidental prediction intended to make a general point about the past and about the present usefulness of therapy. Much of the force of the psychiatric version of their past for the girls, however, came from their very specific understanding of this prediction. And for girls intent upon expressing the House orientation to each other, the view that "unless you understand why this happened, it might happen again" was considered a kind of ace card in persuasion.

During a group therapy discussion of the emotional reasons behind an illegitimate pregnancy, Mary Ann objected, "I know my social worker is always trying to convince me of that. She knows me pretty well, and I think she ought to know me well enough to be able to say if there's a reason, specifically what it is. I keep telling her that it doesn't seem to me to be true and she'll agree, but there's always the implied idea that there was an emotional reason. It's insinuated all the time, in every question. I just keep wondering where the explanation came from to begin with. I mean I wonder what girl they knew well enough to arrive at this idea, this explanation."

Glenda, who rarely spoke, said, "I know I feel that way. I don't think there was any particular reason or way I was treated at home or deep emotional reason for it. I mean— maybe there is, but I don't know if there's always a deep, emotional reason behind this. If there is in my case, I don't know about it."

Lillian said, mostly to Mary Ann, "Do you really think that? I mean, that there was no reason? It would frighten me to think that, because then I wouldn't know why I did it and I might do it again."

Julie said, also to Mary Ann, "I know I felt that way when I came, but I feel now that if you don't know why you're here, you'll end up here again."

＊   ＊   ＊

During a private discussion with Julie in her room, she was talking about the therapy group. She said, "I just didn't feel like saying anything last time. In a way, I guess I feel I've gotten everything I need to get out of the group."

She said, referring to the fact that she had been in the group prior to this one and was therefore one of the longer term members, "You know if I said anything I'd have to say, 'Well, this is the way I felt way back at some time, and this is the way I feel now.' My outlook has changed so much. And the others seem to be back at the stage where I was a long time ago. It just doesn't seem worth the effort.

"When I first came here I had it all figured out in my mind that Tom (her boyfriend) had kind of talked me into it and I gave in. I kind of put it all on him. I didn't really accept my own part in it. I know my brother and I were talking about this yesterday. I was saying how much I had changed and he said that that's one of the reasons why they had wanted me to come to Hawthorne House.

"I know when I first came here they stressed a lot that if you don't realize why you're here or why you ended up here and the emotional reasons behind it, that it will happen again. All the psychiatrists here will tell you that. I know Dr. Hildreth tells you that. Well, I know I thought about it a lot, but I just couldn't see it. I thought about it for a long time. I know Louise [one of her friends in the House] and I came to the same realization the very same week—what our emotional reasons for getting pregnant were. I feel now that I have a pretty full understanding of why I did end up here and that there was an emotional reason for it. And I accept my part in it more. It wasn't just him."

For many girls, therefore, one of the steps in their progress through Hawthorne House was a shift from a disavowal of the past to an avowal of certain features of the past which *accounted* for pregnancy. Yet this avowal of the past was selective in an interesting way, for girls played down their past sexual involvement by seeing it as the manifestation of other, deeper, and nonsexual emotional needs and problems.

During a formally led discussion among about eight girls, Marlene commented, "It's funny. There are a lot of girls here, not in this room but here in the House, who don't want to think that there is anything psychological about what they did. They want to think, 'Well I went out with Joe and I got pregnant.' They don't want to think that there might be a particular reason in themselves, anything psychological about what they did. They just want to think it was Joe and the relationship they had with him. They have such a hard time believing that it is possible that there was any other thing that they wanted. It was just a sex thing to them. That is what they want to believe."

* * *

Peg said, "This is funny—you ask why did it happen to you, why was I the one selected to get back to reality. So many girls go on for years having two or three affairs or maybe it's just their first affair, and they end here, and those who go having affairs for years and years and never have reality brought home to them. I think God has chosen us. I know it sounds corny, but I really think that, because look at the number of girls that could go on for years and years, and never see the reality of what they are doing."

If the girls were willing, even eager, to exchange a *mistake* view of the past for a psychiatric view, this must be understood at least partly in terms of the special comfort of a view which did not merely set aside the past but accounted for it, and accounted for it in ways which allowed girls to believe they would act differently in the future.[1]

1. Jean Thompson's (1967) account of her stay in a Salvation Army home reports a number of conversations among the girls about "why they got pregnant," suggesting that, even in settings which don't sponsor psychiatric explanation, pregnant girls, particularly middle-class girls with a degree of education and an inclination to self-reflection, will construct their own, if less elegant, psychological versions of the past.

The implications girls drew for their future behavior are, in fact, among the most interesting features of their conversion to a psychiatric version of the past.

Dr. Hildreth, in group therapy meeting, said, "There are two problems that all girls who come here face. The first is making a decision about the baby, about what to do with the baby. And the second has to do with the fact that once this behavior exists it may be likely to happen again, unless something changes. The second problem, therefore, is seeing that it doesn't happen again."

No one responded to this, and there was a long silence. Then Pat began by saying, "I know I was talking to my mother about that very thing today. The trouble is that it's so hard to say what you're going to do. I mean, you can make promises and everything, but you don't know what will be possible. . . . It's just so hard to say. . . . I think I'll be able to do it, though, because I found a person that I've become very close to in the course of this situation. He is a wonderful person, and he's taught me that sex is not necessary before marriage, and that you can have a relationship that is deep and real and everything without necessarily having sex. I think with him it will be possible."

                                                        ✿   ✿   ✿

Mrs. Collins looked around the group (a discussion group for the older girls over eighteen) and asked if anybody else had anything to say.

Louise said, "Well, I think that matter of trusting yourself is important. I know girls wonder about going back to their normal lives and think maybe about contraceptives and whether or not they would use them and it's sort of like you wonder whether you trust yourself not to misuse them; and it's sort of like you wonder whether you could have them and use them without feeling that it was a justification for doing things which you do not want yourself to do otherwise. You have to decide whether to trust yourself with that."

Peg reacted, "I know for myself that through this experience I have come much closer to my mother and I feel that I have found a kind of security that I won't be looking for anymore, and I don't need contraceptives.

"I know when I was in the family home the woman there told me why didn't I use contraceptives before. She said she hoped I would rush right out when I left and get a prescription for birth control pills, and I told her that I didn't really want to rush right out and do that.

"I think I should have more trust in myself and feel that I could be strong enough not to have birth control pills around. I mean, if I had the pills around, I would be tempted to do things that I would not want myself to do. In this way I have to be stronger and I think with the love and security I've found since I got pregnant, I can do this."

❊　❊　❊

A record called "The Case for Chastity" was played in the discussion group to stimulate discussion. After the record, the group worker asked for reactions.

Ardis said, "I liked the explanation about why we got pregnant, about the business of looking for love. That was new to me, and it seems like a good idea." This led to a brief discussion of looking for love via sex.

Ruth then said, "Anyway, you can know why you're doing something but it doesn't necessarily change it. But I guess if you know, then the next time you feel this kind of need coming on, you can seek professional help."

On one level, the girls' sexually conservative intentions for the future had less to do with the psychiatric view of their situation per se than with their own ambivalence toward sexual involvement, an ambivalence tipped in a conservative direction by the trouble of pregnancy. In this sense, it is not surprising that the girls should reach much the same conclusion from a psychiatric view of their situation as they would from a more straightforward, although less elegant, version of their past behavior as a *mistake*.

Yet, on another level, the girls' intentions must be understood in terms of the House orientations and operation. On the one hand, many staff members did not oppose premarital sexual relations and, in fact, strongly urged girls to get a prescription for birth control pills or some self-provided and self-controlled means of contraception. On the other hand, these opinions were expressed privately and individually as part of the therapeutic relationship and were secondary to the more general purposes of therapy. The staff did not therefore systematically and publicly condone premarital sexual relations, nor, given the natural reservation that the acceptability of premarital sexual activity depends on the girl and the circumstances, did the staff publicly take this more moderate stance.

One cannot escape observing that, even if unintentional, one of the consequences of the psychiatric emphasis at Hawthorne House was to remove from official concern the moral question raised by the girls' illegitimate pregnancies.

The most obvious benefit of not treating this question directly is that the staff were frequently faced with justifying their institution and its practices to a quite conservative public. This point can be most dramatically made by an excerpt from one of the meetings held intermittently with interested parents of girls currently in the House. While the father quoted was later viewed with horrified astonishment on the part of the staff members, his views simply represented in a caricatured way the feelings common to many of the parents present and, by extension, the feelings of much of the House's public. What is more important, the policies of the House could be easily stated so as to defuse his possible objections.

A man sitting toward the front said, "Well, we know that this is not acceptable behavior. Of course, my wife and I will accept the girl back in the family if she returns alone. But I wonder about this acceptance of what they have done. She knows that what she has done is unacceptable in the eyes of society, but I wondered what you do in the home in the way of teaching sexual responsibility. I mean, do you have question and answer periods, or explain how this is viewed by society, or anything of that sort? We wonder about these things because we wonder where did we fail."

Mrs. Lewin said, "I think we feel that most girls know that it is unacceptable or they wouldn't be here. You know they wouldn't come to a place like this unless they felt that way. We take the position as an organization that we are neither condemning nor condoning, but we have set up our program to help the girl understand why she has come here. . . . We have group discussions and psychological help and caseworkers, and through all these means we try to help the girl to understand why she got herself into this situation."

The man said, "How do you feel about girls returning to dating?"

Mrs. Lewin looked at him, then said, "How do you feel?"

He said, "Confused," and went on to say a few things which implied that he was against his daughter going back to dating. The social workers present all reacted negatively to this.

Mrs. Lewin said, "We expect girls will resume their heterosexual relationships in the manner of dating, but we feel that if they have learned something during their stay here, they can communicate better with their parents and they don't need to act out in inappropriate ways."

A second advantage of not officially addressing the moral issue of premarital sexual relations was that this allowed staff members of varying moral persuasions or degrees of uncertainty to coexist and operate constructively in areas of less ambiguity. Even so, it is interesting that one staff member, long affiliated with the House and thoroughly committed to a psychiatric view of the girls, reported being called on the carpet once, for remarking, on psychological grounds, that for many girls it was not a matter of if, but when, girls would get pregnant again. The remark was viewed as objectionable because it implied that the girls would resume sexual relations.

The girls' conservative conclusions for the future were therefore not just born of their own ambivalence and concerns for jeopardized respectability but were allowed and somewhat unintentionally supported by the House psychiatric orientation. And it is interesting in this regard that those few girls who actively resisted and objected to a psychiatric view of their past were also the girls who actively and openly accepted and argued in favor of premarital sexual relations.

For most girls however, and in spite of staff intentions, conversion to a psychiatric view of the past partly resolved the issue of jeopardized respectability by providing an acceptable, that is nonsexual, interpretation of the past and a set of related new resolves for the future.

TIMETABLES AND MORAL CAREER

The conception of an institutional career has usually been used as a way of pointing to the shifting contingencies and concerns persons experience as they enter an institution, come to terms with what they find there, and then anticipate leaving. At Hawthorne House, however, the notion of career is doubly relevant, for a girl's course through the institution was paralleled by her course through pregnancy.

The girls' concerns, expectations, and emotions were closely geared to a timetable[2] constructed around the predicted due date, and this timetable charted a course through pregnancy and through the House. The experience of career was further consolidated by the routines of the House which not only provided the girls with the materials for judging their progress through pregnancy, but which made that progress a salient dimension of their experiences in the institution. The purpose of this section is to describe the organization of careers through the House as a way of locating and characterizing the girls' changing concerns as they approached delivery.

Girls stayed at Hawthorne House for varying lengths of time depending on how early in pregnancy they entered the House. Once a girl delivered, she could expect to spend six days in the hospital and two days back at Hawthorne House. The central indeterminacy was therefore the date of delivery. While the growth and delivery of a baby is irreversible, inevitable, and certain within some predictable time span, many factors such as lack of knowledge of the date of conception and the physical state of the mother combine to make the date of delivery somewhat indeterminate. The due date predicted by the medical staff for each girl could therefore only be a rough estimation of the actual delivery date; the large number of births which occurred more than a week

2. I have taken the concept of "timetables" and the notion of "bench marks" from Julius A. Roth's (1963) study of TB patients. TB patients, faced with a long and indeterminate stay in the hospital, manage the uncertainties of their situation by developing group norms for measuring their progress and take some events as the symbolic, if not actual, bench marks of that progress. Unwed mothers are also concerned with marking time; unlike TB patients, their careers are more determined, having a predictable end point. Yet, like TB patients, unwed mothers treat the end point as more fixed than it actually is and take the predicted end point as the standard for judging their actual progress.

before or after the predicted due date attest to the tentativeness of the prediction.

The emphasis on the due date pervaded daily life in the House. New girls were introduced in the weekly House meetings and in the weekly newspaper by their name and due date, and the due date was perhaps the most common piece of social knowledge girls had about each other. Partly because girls new to the House tended to make friends with others who were new, but also because they sought out others at the same stage, friendships were organized roughly in terms of due date. The weekly newspaper, in listing the births for the preceding week, listed not only the sex and weight of the baby and the date of delivery, but also whether the baby was delivered early, late, or on time (within a week on either side of the due date).

In addition, a number of House rules were defined in terms of a girl's progress toward her due date. Girls with less than six weeks to their due date were no longer eligible for election to one of the many offices in the House. Girls with less than four weeks to predicted delivery could no longer take overnight leaves, nor go on long or unaccompanied trips. And girls were no longer assigned kitchen duties in the final two weeks. While these rules were trivial in one sense, they nevertheless served to mark officially and automatically the girls' progress through the House.

The weekly medical clinic, however, was the central context for marking the girls' progress through pregnancy and through the House. The medical clinic was set up in ways which provided girls with an automatic sense of their progress. Like most pregnant women, girls were examined more frequently as they approached delivery; girls attended the medical clinic once a month, then every two weeks, and finally every week. The medical clinic processed girls in groups according to the week in which the due date fell, so that girls in their thirty-ninth or *final* week were seen first, girls in their thirty-eighth week second, and so on. Furthermore, girls in their final week were no longer seen by any one of the clinic doctors but by Dr. Rodman, the head of the clinic —the group, therefore, came to be known as Dr. Rodman's group and was special certification of the nearness of delivery.

For girls making normal physical progress, therefore, the medical clinic served to mark off that progress week by week. What is more interesting, however, is that girls took the due date as the measure against which they judged their physical progress. On clinic day girls gathered for tea and the exchange of clinic "news." While good and bad clinic news could involve anything from excessive weight gain or excess fluid which might require bed rest, to a possible breech position of the baby, the way girls defined good and bad news was strictly in terms of normal progress toward the due date.

In order to understand the following quotes, it is necessary to know that physical progress toward delivery occurs and is judged by the following order of events: normal weight gain of the baby, *dipping* as the baby begins to turn and move head down toward the eventual delivery position, *engaged* as the baby's head becomes firmly fixed in the delivery position against the cervix, *dilation* as the cervix gradually expands in preparation for delivery, and finally painless contractions which become more frequent and more painful as labor begins and progresses.

In one of the waiting rooms there was a discussion among Mary Ann, myself and Billie. They were both saying that there was a long list of things they wanted to ask the doctor. They wanted to ask if they were *engaged*.

Mary Ann said, "I only ask one thing when I go in there, and that they can't answer. The only thing I keep asking them is will it be born near August 12th, and I know they can't answer that. But I keep forgetting all the other questions. That's the only one I care about. I've asked that three times once, then I forget the others. I shouldn't ask, because they can't answer it anyway."

Mary Ann went in eventually, and came back looking extremely downcast, immediately lit a cigarette, and sat down. She said, "They say the baby is four to six weeks behind now. They said he was behind before, but I didn't know it was that far. They asked if I were sure of my conception date—they seemed to think that maybe it wasn't right. And then they said he was small, about five pounds. All I kept asking was, 'Is that big enough to be born August 12th?'" She was quite upset.

* * *

Emily came back into the waiting room after seeing the doctor, on the verge of tears. She said, "Well I'm on everything this week—partial bed rest, phenobarb, six iron pills a meal, you name it. Fluid pills—and they say the baby is only 36 weeks."

Someone asked, "What are you?"

She said, "The end of the week begins my 38th week. I said to them 'I've been here too long—forever. I have to get out by then.' Boy, wait till I tell my mother. I called home last week and said I was *engaged*. She said, 'Are you engaged to Donald again?' I said, 'No—the baby. The baby's head is engaged.' So this week I'll call back and say that nothing is engaged, me or the baby. It can't be true."

She was almost crying and Shirley sympathetically squeezed her hand.

While the due date therefore operated as the measure by which girls assessed their own normal progress, it was also the measure by which girls judged and controlled each others' hopes and anxieties. For while girls might hope to deliver *early,* girls did not allow each other to *expect* to deliver early; nor did they allow each other to object to someone else's good luck.

Waiting down in the clinic, Julie remarked to me in a low tone, "I get so upset by some of these girls that get so upset when they don't get good news in clinic even though they haven't even gotten to their due date yet. I know Kim was down here and she took it so hard when they told her nothing had happened yet. And she's not even due. I didn't think she was really in proportion. She shouldn't get so upset. Sandy has been so good about it, even though she's a couple of weeks overdue. She doesn't complain or get upset or anything."

Later Julie was talking to Marlene, saying something about superstition. I said, "What's all this about superstition?"

Julie said, "I was just telling Marlene that a long time ago when someone broke their water and went two weeks early, Kim said 'I hope she comes back.' Well I never heard anyone say that before. No matter how early someone goes, you're always glad when they go to the hospital, and you never hope she comes back. It just seemed like such an unusual thing that I think it was kind of superstitious for Kim."

*   *   *

Waiting for the group therapy meeting to assemble, Susan was commenting on a new girl in the House, "She really did a terrible thing the other day. You know Marlene was sent back from the hospital and she was sitting around the snack kitchen with some other girls. This girl came in and was telling her she was a reject. I guess she said that because at dinner Marlene had been sitting at the table where she was a waitress; Marlene was kidding around about sending her doughnut back because it had a hole in it—she said, 'Take back this reject.' So this girl was teasing Marlene about being a reject from the hospital. No one knew quite what to say. We all expected Marlene to come back with a sore retort like she usually does, but she didn't. She just sat there. And then every time this girl saw Marlene she would kid her about being a reject.

"Finally, I said something to her. I explained how the girls feel if they've been waiting all this time and then go over to the hospital and are sent back—that it's not the kind of thing you joke about. She just shrugged her shoulders. I don't know if she understood or not. She's really something."

*　*　*

I went to clinic and sat in the new little room which is off the hall. Dr. Rodman's group was gathered there. They were discussing who would be taken to the hospital. As each girl left to see the doctor, the others would speculate on whether or not she would be taken, then wait for her return and the news.

When Dora was in seeing Dr. Rodman, Beverly said, "I hope he doesn't take her. Not really. I hope he does. I just wish he would take us both. We wanted to go together." Beverly was mad at Dr. Rodman because he wasn't going to take her. She kept saying, "I dilated two. How much do you have to dilate to go? I thought he would take me today."

When I was upstairs later, I heard several girls commenting on Beverly, on how mad she was at not being taken. Someone said, "When is she due?"

Someone else said, "Not yet, next Tuesday."

Then someone said, "Well, then why is she so upset?"

The importance girls placed on normal progress and delivering *on time*, if not early, must be understood in terms of the variety of hopes and anxieties which were tied to delivery and accentuated by House orientations and routines. These will be described in terms of the high turnover of clients in the House, anxiety over labor which increases as the due date approaches, and increasing anticipation and anxiety over becoming a mother.

The girls' sense of the passage of time, particularly as the due date approaches, was given a special quality by the high turnover in the House. The turnover was high enough so that both the staff and the girls had to resort, on occasion, to descriptions to identify a particular girl for someone else. While girls experienced the turnover from the beginning of their stay at Hawthorne House, it became most salient when friends left, when roommates left, and when girls with approximately the same due date started leaving, whether early or on time.

During group therapy meeting, Mona said, "I feel kind of lost now. It seems like everybody is going over. My roommate went, and a lot of people I know have gone to the hospital. And it seems kind of lonely, and you don't know what to do. It seems like I spent so much time expecting for everyone else, and now there's nobody to expect for. I know I felt this way about my roommate. I expected for her for so long, and then she left and now there's not much to do. There's six girls gone this week."

Kim said, "Some of these girls—I didn't believe they would ever go. I didn't believe Sandy would go. I thought she had a case of permanent pregnancy."

Marlene said, "Well, now it's my turn. I'm next on the list."

Kim said, "Well Amelia is next after you. Then there is the next group due next week—Jerri and someone else."

❊   ❊   ❊

During the House Council meeting, someone mentioned room changes. Shirley said, "Yeah, people are lining up way ahead of time now. I've got somebody who's waiting for my room when I leave right now." She said something about people coming and taking things out as if she had already left. "I feel like I should really be on my way."

The combined effect of loss of friends, retirement from House activities as they become repetitive (for example, prenatal classes, discussions devoted to points of view already taken, decisions already made), or as officeholding expires, increasing confinement to the House, and increasing physical discomfort as sleep becomes more difficult and the weight of the baby more wearing—all these things combined to intensify the quality of private waiting as the due date approached.

In a private discussion with Julie in her room, she said, "I just couldn't get involved in the discussion this morning. Usually, I'm right with them, but somehow this morning I just didn't even feel like going. I've been patient for so long, but now it just seems like I'm impatient and getting tired of waiting. I knew when I was at my brother's last week, I really felt as if that was my last dinner forever."

I asked, "Is it because that was the last time you could go there, or was it because of the beginning of the last three weeks?"

She said, "I guess because it's the beginning of the last three weeks. I'm getting very impatient now. It seems funny because I came in early—earlier than most girls—but I haven't minded at all. I've had plenty to do, lots of things to keep me occupied, but now I'm just not interested. Like the other day, I went to the beach with my girlfriend and her boyfriend, and usually I'd like that a lot, but I was just so tired of being stared at. And I saw all the girls in two-piece bathing suits, and I felt like wearing my regular clothes. I didn't even enjoy it. And like this morning, I fell asleep for awhile which I don't normally do. I just don't want to do anything. I guess it will probably pass in a day or so, and I'll be busy doing things again. But right now I just don't feel much like doing anything."

These were experiences which in some measure the girls shared with pregnant women in general; and they shared with other women pregnant for the first time special anxieties over labor and delivery. Institutionalized unwed mothers, however, are probably exposed more routinely and thoroughly to information and to the actual beginnings of labor than are most pregnant women. Girls, in their desire not to be sent back from the hospital preferred to wait until their labor pains were regular and frequent before leaving for the hospital. Girls timing labor pains were thus a common sight in the House. The constant presence of a nurse who answered questions both in formal prenatal classes and informally added to girls' knowledge.

While this constant flow of information about pregnancy was soothing in the sense that girls knew what to expect, it also exposed girls to graphic accounts of delivery by those returning to the House. Girls returning generally tended to monitor their accounts except in the presence of friends or other girls who had also delivered. Yet the inevitable sifting of these accounts into the House reinforced the anxiety girls already felt.

In an informal conversation Kit, new to the House, mentioned being scared of labor and delivery. A bit later she said, to the others sitting around, "Well, they knock you out. You don't feel anything anyways, do you?" This was quite a different version from what I had been hearing around the House, and it seemed to me the others sitting around were reluctant to say otherwise.

Jerri had said earlier, "The girls around here are pretty

good about coming back and telling people things. They don't make it seem rosy hued, but they don't exaggerate it, or go into a lot of detail."

In response to Kit's remark, Julie then said, "Well you feel it a fair amount, but they give you a drug which makes you kind of hazy, and they give you a drug which makes you forget about it afterwards."

Kit said, "I guess you forget all the pain anyway, afterwards, but it sounds kind of scary."

❋   ❋   ❋

Several girls in the group-therapy meeting, which had by now decreased from fifteen to five, had attended a joint meeting of soon-to-deliver and postpartum girls. At that meeting several girls had recounted their deliveries in vivid detail. Lillian had told me how upset she, Ann, Emily, and Glenda (the prenatals) had been over it. Now, in group-therapy meeting she brought up the subject again, saying how upset she and the others had been. She then asked Claire, who had delivered and just returned to the group-therapy meeting, "Tell us what some of the nice experiences are."

Finally, it must be observed that while to some extent the girls shared these anxieties with other pregnant women, particularly those pregnant for the first time, they faced labor and delivery without the immediate support of family or husband.

BECOMING A MOTHER

The central feature of a girl's career through Hawthorne House, and the central feature of her moral career in becoming an unwed mother, was, however, her increasing involvement with her baby, with becoming a mother. The girls'

initial concern with respectability, expressed in relief at rescue from potential public shame and in a subsequent interest
in a psychiatric view of the past, gradually gave way to other
concerns and other ways of defining their situation.

From an initial inclination on the part of many girls entering the House to minimize their attachment to the baby,
most girls shifted to a wish for greater attachment. In the
ways which were described in the preceding chapter, this
shift was expressed in their conversion to an intention to see
and feed their babies and, for some girls, in a real ambivalence about adoption. In lesser ways too, the girls expressed
their growing involvement with their babies. Girls new to the
House and relatively early in pregnancy, for example, were
frequently put off by the demeanor and everyday talk of the
older girls who poked and pushed their *stomachs* and made
remarks about their babies' activities, sometimes mock-
addressing these remarks to the babies. While the girls could
express their growing involvement to some extent during
pregnancy, their major decisions and greatest involvement
could only be expressed following delivery, and then for only
a short time. They could not, for example, express their involvement during pregnancy in the usual preparations for
bringing a baby home. Their sense of attachment therefore
became increasingly directed toward delivery, and specifically toward their due date.

Girls looked forward to delivery with an increasing anticipation and anxiety as they approached the due date, for they
looked forward simultaneously to having the baby and giving it up. Even girls firm in their resolve about adoption were
aware of the persistent observation among the girls that
"girls change their minds in the hospital," a rumor supported
by the avid interest in the House when a girl who had been
planning to have the baby adopted changed her mind. What
girls came to consider their most difficult decisions and cen-

tral concerns during their stay at Hawthorne House could therefore not be expressed until delivery.

Thus, the timetable the girls constructed around the predicted date of delivery charted a course through pregnancy and through the House and a course of concerns and emotions increasingly directed toward delivery, at which time the girls' experiences and the structure of the House combined to define them as transformed from pregnant girls to mothers.

THE RETURN OF MOTHERS TO THE HOUSE

I will not attempt to describe directly the girls' experiences of labor, delivery, and days with their babies in the hospital. An account of what the girls themselves felt to be an intense and private experience would inevitably be inadequate; in addition, although I paid hospital visits to girls I regarded as friends and in whose company I had spent a fair amount of time, I regarded even these visits as an intrusion which I could not justify to myself on the grounds of sociological curiosity. I felt the grace with which girls at Hawthorne House had accepted my presence deserved this consideration for their privacy. In doing this, I make the same distinction between girls awaiting delivery and mothers that was made by the staff, the procedures of the House, and the girls themselves.

Upon entering the House, girls were assigned to rooms as beds became available. When a girl left for the hospital, her belongings were packed and labeled; on her return from the hospital she was assigned a room, usually a single room, in a special section of the House reserved for mothers. This section was removed from the main social gathering areas. In addition, some rules were suspended while other rules became applicable. For example, girls were no longer required to attend breakfast but, for medical reasons, were not allowed to leave the grounds without special arrangement.

While some distinctions made between mothers and other girls were medically based, many were not, and in making these other distinctions (like the room arrangement), Hawthorne House both recognized and defined the returning girls' change of status. Mothers were viewed seriously.

During a staff discussion of the advisability of recommending that girls stay longer in the House following their return from the hospital, possibly ten days, several case-workers objected. Mrs. Hilton said, "I don't think it's such a good idea anyway. They've just undergone a tremendous loss and I think in times of loss people want to be with their families, even if their families don't always provide them with much help. It's a time of mourning, and I don't think it's very helpful to be around here with a bunch of prenatals running around."

The change girls felt in themselves was reflected in the strangeness they expressed in returning to the House, and the distance they felt now lay between themselves and even their friends who were still waiting. These feelings of strangeness and distance were compounded of a feeling that the major events and topics of discussion in the House were no longer relevant, a feeling that they should not, could not, or might not wish to describe their experiences to girls in the House. Girls felt embarrassed at no longer being pregnant in the company of those who were. And finally they felt a sense of relief and fulfillment at actually feeling what was expected—joy in motherhood, sorrow in loss, and a genuine concern for the baby.

After the girls who had come up to welcome Peg back to the House had left, Peg and I were still standing in the hall. She had asked me earlier if there was any place we could get some tea or coffee. Her question really surprised me because she knows the House as well as I do. It seemed to reflect her new status as a mother returning to the House for a visit, not really being part of it.

In the snack kitchen, she said, "I feel like a stranger here. I don't know anyone anymore. It seems so funny." While we were sitting there several girls passed the door; Peg went to the door at one point, then came back and said, "I shouldn't really go out there. I know the girls who are passing by the door hate seeing me. I know that's how I'd feel, how I did feel. You hate to see girls come back from the hospital. Maybe that's why they separate them and put them way off in a separate place. You talk to them at first. I remember when I was first in the House, I'd rush up to any girl who came back from the hospital and ask all about it. But then you stop doing it. It makes you feel crummy. They're all finished."

Later at dinner I noticed Peg had changed from the tight-fitting dress she had on earlier to a smock. She said, "I just felt too out of place. I had to change."

*   *   *

During lunch, the discussion was mainly between Marlene and Pat who had both delivered and returned to the House to spend their last few days. Marlene was quite animated over her recent decision to keep her baby; Pat was pale and miserable, her decision being very much up in the air.

Pat said, "It's so terrible. All these people rush up and say 'Hi' and want to talk and everything, and I just don't even feel like it. Even with my friends. I just don't even feel like saying 'Hi'." She looked quite sad, pale, and weary.

Marlene said, "Didn't I tell you you'd get tired of being asked 'How do you feel?' That's all they ask you everywhere you go. . . . Then you get some of the new ones that rush up and say 'What's it like?' and they have ten weeks to go." She sounded amazed and a little derisive. "If somebody came up to me who was almost ready to go to the hospital and asked what it was like, I would tell them all about it. What can you tell someone with ten weeks left though? You've got a long time ahead of you."

I asked Pat, "Why does it seem so funny to be back?"

She said, "I don't know. You just can't talk to anybody. You don't have anything in common anymore."

Marlene said, somewhat exaggeratedly and kiddingly, "You're a mother now." Then she said more seriously, "You are."

Pat said, "You've been through so much. How can you tell someone what it's like? It's so beautiful when you see the baby coming out and everything. It's just such a beautiful experience. I think I felt then that I had done more than I have ever done in my life all added up. I was never so happy as that moment. I can't explain it."

Marlene agreed, "It is beautiful. You feel like a mother."

Girls felt themselves transformed by the experience of becoming a mother to the extent that their past concerns with secrecy, with hiding the fact of pregnancy, now seemed unimportant, if necessary. Taken over by their experience, girls wished to share the force of it with others—with friends at home, with their families. For the experience of becoming a mother seemed to girls returning to the House to eclipse fully the experience of being illegitimately pregnant.

During my hospital visit with Jerri, she talked at one point about still being somewhat fat and having to get rid of it so people wouldn't suspect when she went home. Then she said, "But somehow, after you go through all of this and spend all this time and go through it all, you don't really care so much anymore. You've just been through too

much to care if somebody finds out. You sort of feel—
what difference does it make?"

    ❃   ❃   ❃

In the over-eighteen discussion group, Pat anticipated
how she would feel after delivering and going home, "I
just have the feeling that the things I used to do and like
to do are going to bore me now . . . like I just think if somebody called me up and said, 'Come on over, we're having
a party' I wouldn't want to go. . . . I guess it seems like, of
all the people I know, I will have changed more than anyone else. They will have changed some in a year, but I will
have changed a lot more. So I won't feel like doing the
same things I used to do. . . ."

    ❃   ❃   ❃

Peg commented, "I just really want to tell someone
about it. It's such a big thing and it was so marvelous. It
seems funny not to tell someone."

RETURNING HOME

Whatever resolves and remembrances, whatever definition of her situation a girl drew for herself from her experiences in becoming an unwed mother at Hawthorne House,
she faces upon her return home other definitions of her situation, as well as an impending reinvolvement with her usual
home concerns.

Few girls returned to a home situation in which their true
situation was not known about by anyone. Hawthorne House
required parental knowledge as a condition of entrance except in very unusual circumstances; additionally, many girls
had told or would tell close friends. Furthermore, from the
accounts of girls who came back to the House for the six-
week medical checkup, it seems that as girls became rein-

volved in dating they felt some special pressure to reveal their past to the boys they dated as a way of staving off sexual involvement, perhaps thereby substituting one form of closeness for another.

Girls' relations with others were complicated by the double quality of their past experiences, and the different expectations they faced in relating to those who knew and those who did not know their true situation. In themselves, the girls felt two ways about their past situation—happy and proud of the experience of becoming a mother, and yet they also mourned the loss of the baby. For others who did not know their situation, the girls had to act convincingly normal and happy and had to provide an adequate account of their imaginary experiences in the preceding months. For those who did know, the girls were assumed to be unhappy and treated as if they were.

In relation to those who knew, the girls could not easily express the joyfulness of their experience, for at the times they wished to speak of the happy event it was, they faced persons who at that moment were more likely to treat the experience as the loss it also was. And in the face of others' efforts, particularly parental efforts, to cheer them up and to distract them from grief neither could they easily express their sorrow.[3]

3. In expressing their true feelings to those who knew, girls faced the interactional difficulties which normally confront the bereaved.

"It is a central feature of the bereavement situation that the rule-governed character of expressive behavior is precisely its more problematic aspect. In the routinization of contacts between bereaved and non bereaved persons we see continuous work involved in the adjustment of actual feelings to the conditions of concrete interactional situations, wherein there is a considerable amount both of underplaying and overplaying of expressive demonstration, required to handle the conditions of interaction between parties holding varying perspectives toward the death" (Sudnow, 1967 : 140).

These difficulties were additionally complicated by the ambiguity of the loss (in some respects it had been a happy event, and the girls had, after all, chosen adoption), and complicated by the existence of others who did not know and could not be told.

In postpartum meeting, Dr. Hildreth asked Sandy more about her not being able to talk at home. She said, "Well I just get the feeling that they want me to forget about it and put it out of my mind. It's never that they tell me not to talk about it, but it's just that whenever I say anything, they kind of listen and then the conversation drops. I think it's their idea that if I don't talk about it, I won't think about it, but that isn't true."

                    *   *   *

In the postpartum meeting, Marcia said, "My mother is always finding something for me to do. can't be alone in the room for two minutes without her coming in and asking me if I want to embroider or something. I have all this stuff left over from when I was here—two dresses I haven't finished, embroidery, all kinds of stuff. I've got plenty to do."

Louise said, "I know. My mother keeps babying me. I almost struck out at her last week and I was ashamed of myself. I know I should understand the way she feels about it, but I can't even read a book without her worrying, and she uses this kind of baby-talk I can't stand. . . ."

Darlene said, "I keep going out all the time so I won't have to be around."

Dr. Hildreth commented, "You are all feeling uncomfortable with your parents then."

Darlene said, "Not uncomfortable so much as embarrassed, particularly around my father. I don't know, it just embarrasses me."

Girl's relations with those who knew were further complicated by the stance they had to take toward those who did not know, frequently in the company of those who did. For in acting convincingly normal and happy, girls not only risked demeaning their own loss but also presented themselves as competent liars.

In the postpartum meeting, Marcia said, "Well, my girl-friend and her mother know about it, and my girlfriend told me that her mother didn't exactly approve of the way I was acting. She thought I was acting too happy, and that I didn't learn my lesson."

*   *   *

In the evening meeting for girls who had delivered and gone home, Louise said at one point, "It's all right with the people who know for sure and with the people who don't know. It's the people who you're not sure about that really get you. You don't know whether to tell your 'story' and then feel like a fool because they already know about it, or whether to tell them the truth when you didn't have to. And then you sort of feel foolish when there's some-body that does know and you're telling the 'story' to some-body else."

Furthermore, the care with which the girls' families main-tained the public fiction and attempted to erase the past, if only for the sake of their daughters, served as a source of more general shame. In this situation, there lay the possibili-ties both of increased closeness within the family out of shared complicity and feelings and of a degree of cynicism about the high price paid to avoid potential public shame.

A girl's gradual reinvolvement in usual and normal activi-ties eventually raised the prospect of dating and concerns which had become suspended during pregnancy. In her return to sexual respectability, although now somewhat devalued in importance by the force of her experience in be-coming a mother, a girl could make a fresh start. Many girls reported being nervous about the prospect of resuming dat-ing, and said they felt it would be like their first date again. This first-date quality suggests rather clearly the complete moral reinstatement girls experienced; girls' conservative intentions for their future sexual behavior, eclipsed by other concerns toward the end of pregnancy, became relevant once again as dating raised old issues.

In terms of the argument made in the first chapter, it could be said that one consequence of the moral reprieve intentionally or unintentionally offered to unwed mothers is to return them to the stage of sexual involvement and the set of ambivalences in which pregnancy is maximally risked. In this sense, I would agree with the psychiatric staff at Hawthorne House, although for different reasons, that girls are likely to become sexually involved again in much the same ways they did before pregnancy and are likely to risk pregnancy in much the same ways.

To some extent, a girl's reinvolvement in sexual activity may be changed by her past experience for she is not only aware of the past but may retain the marks of her past experience on her body—in the form of "stretch-marks" on her breasts or stomach. In this sense, her gradual reinvolvement in sexual activity not only jeopardizes sexual respectability in the usual ways but also her past moral status as well as her more recent presentation of self.

It was perhaps against this contingency and sense of fraudulent status that girls felt compelled to confess the past, and that virtually every girl at Hawthorne House affirmed an intention to confess to the man she would love and marry. But in confessing the past, girls were once again open to old debates—between love and desire, on the one hand, and reputation and a sense of respectability, on the other.

While a girl's sense of moral reinstatement thus became somewhat evanescent as she once again faced familiar decisions, and experienced familiar evasions of sexual intention, she could look back on the experience of becoming a mother as the central and most meaningful definition of her experience of becoming an unwed mother.

III

Accommodations to Illegitimacy

5

The Project

> While the initial planners of the project were convinced that medical and mental health services for these girls should be given major attention, they decided that offering the girls an opportunity to participate in an accredited school program was basic to insuring their involvement in the total project.
>
> From a published description of the Project, written by its director.

The Project was, at the time I studied it, a small temporary "pilot" school for unwed mothers located in the black ghetto of a large city in the Midwest. Publicly financed for a limited time, the Project was designed to dramatize the necessity and possibility of providing services for young Negro pregnant girls—girls who usually keep their illegitimate babies and who ordinarily do not come to the attention of social agencies. The Project was, at this time, jointly sponsored by the city's boards of mental health and education. In ways that will become evident, this division in sponsorship was reflected in the practical operation of the Project, as well as in its effect on the girls who came there.

The services provided by the Project took the form of a grade school run expressly for the Project girls, group and individual counseling of the girls and their families, and the arrangement of regular prenatal care with the public clinics of the city.

The Project staff was small, consisting at this time of nine persons. Of these, only four had much to do with the girls themselves—two teachers, one Negro, one white; the social worker, Negro; and a psychiatric nurse, white.[1]

The main office of the Project was in several rooms of a public housing project; the school was located in a room of a YWCA several blocks away. The social worker conducted private interviews at the main office, notably the intake interview with each girl and her mother required for entrance into the Project school. Most of the girls' experiences with the Project, however, occurred at the school. Both the social worker and the psychiatric nurse came to the school to conduct their weekly group meetings with the girls. The teachers spent their days at the school, only occasionally going to the headquarters location.

Originally, Project participation was limited to Negro girls in elementary school (through eighth grade) who were interested in continuing their education during and following their pregnancies. Many of these girls had been held back in school and were somewhat old for their grade; most girls were about fourteen years old—young to be pregnant. The girls were predominantly from lower-class families; of the girls who had participated in the Project over the three years of its existence, about half lived in one-parent homes and about a third were themselves illegitimate.

1. I myself am white, a fact which appeared to interfere less with my relations to the Project girls at the time than with my later sense of having accurately understood their concerns and world view. More generally, at Hawthorne House I ran the sociological dangers of studying persons like myself; on the Project I ran the anthropological dangers of studying persons much unlike myself. While the first situation is more likely to support the illusion of accuracy, I do not know which situation favors greater accuracy in fact.

The Project required that the girl's family, usually her mother, be agreeable to her participation; mothers were urged to attend the twice-monthly evening meetings of mothers with the social worker and were required to accompany their daughters for the intake interview.

The Project accepted girls in their first illegitimate pregnancy not beyond their seventh month. These girls continued to live at home, commuting daily to the school. Virtually all planned to, and did, keep their babies although the social worker consistently raised the possibilities of adoptive or foster home placement.

The capacity of the Project was limited, largely by the size of the classroom, to a maximum of about thirty-five girls at a time. Usually fewer than this were actually attending school for there were always girls out awaiting or recovering from delivery after which they returned to finish out the semester. In this respect, the Project was less strictly geared to pregnancy than most settings for unwed mothers in which the girl's involvement essentially ends with delivery.

I spent about four months in the winter and spring of 1966 on the Project, participant-observing and later interviewing. My concerns, methods, and problems are presented in the Appendix. Very generally speaking, I sat in the classroom, watched and listened, talked with girls in their spare moments, ate lunch with them, attended their group-therapy-style meetings, and went places with them after school—trying, in this way, to see what spontaneously concerned them. At about the time when schoolroom observation was becoming less useful in terms of increased understanding, the school was moved to a church and gradually expanded to include high-school girls. Grades were separated and more teachers were employed. The classes became more organized and the kind of informal private conversations that had occurred in the one-room-schoolhouse atmosphere of the "Y" were less possible. During this time I began to interview girls more formally after school, while still participating in those school activities where conversation was still possible.

There were few formal staff meetings at the time of my presence on the Project, and my observations of the staff were largely limited to their encounters with the girls, although I did have private conversations with staff members on occasion.

PROJECT OBJECTIVES

Like other settings for unwed mothers, the Project provided a number of practical, needed-for-the-moment services which helped tide girls over some of the immediate problems raised by an illegitimate pregnancy. The school kept girls from falling behind and also restored a familiar pattern to daily life. Regular medical attention and discussions of pregnancy and birth allayed some of the girls' fears, at least some of their uncertainties. And the company of other girls in the same situation, and of staff members familiar with this situation, provided support and advice for more specific problems with families, boyfriends, or babies.

Unlike many settings for unwed mothers, however, the Project recruited girls who not only would not ordinarily receive these services, but whose age and background made these services especially important. In this sense, the Project staff could and did feel a special sense of purpose in simply providing these for-the-moment services. Yet the Project staff hoped not only to guide girls through the immediate problems of an illegitimate pregnancy, but also to have more long-term effects on their clients.

Specifically, the Project staff hoped to reduce the likelihood of a second illegitimate pregnancy and to extend the length of time girls remained in school following the birth of a child. More generally, the Project staff hoped, through such means as group and individual counseling, to bring about some changes in the girls' understanding of their situations which would then be reflected in the more specific ways mentioned.

These more long-term purposes involved, then, both a set of etiological understandings about the sources of illegitimate pregnancy and a set of related notions as to what must be changed and how. On the Project, these etiological and treatment notions were blended of conceptions about illegitimate pregnancy and conceptions about lower-class Negro life.

On the one hand, the Project was designed and headed by professional social workers who were inclined by their training to view illegitimate pregnancy as the result of certain psychological needs, certain characteristic ways of handling problems. Pregnant girls, viewed this way, should be helped to understand their motivations, needs, and characteristic patterns of behavior lest their situation reoccur in the future.

On the other hand, the Project staff were concerned with the more general problems of being poor and black—problems not specifically tied to illegitimate pregnancy and with origins outside the particular psychological arrangements of any one family. From this perspective, girls should be helped to acquire the knowledge and skills to take control of their lives.

The rest of this chapter has to do with the ways in which these general purposes were more specifically expressed by various staff members and with the ways the girls who came to the Project understood these expressions.

THE STAFF

The staff members who had routine contact with the girls were the teachers, the social worker, and the psychiatric nurse. Much of the possible impact of the Project was diluted, whether desirably or undesirably, by the noninvolve-

ment of the teachers in the larger and longer-range orientations of the Project.

While the teachers had the greatest amount of contact
with the Project girls, their primary commitment was to
teaching and they were relatively unconcerned with their
pupils' out-of-class lives. The problems they faced from day
to day were the problems of teachers in general: gaining and
keeping control of the class, enforcing classroom rules, and
getting through the material as planned. While each of the
teachers expressed an interest in working with *socially mal-
adjusted* or *problem* kids, this interest had less to do with the
girls' pregnancies than with their coming from low-income,
impoverished backgrounds and having bad academic and
truancy records.

This emphasis on the strictly teaching aspects of their
Project position was intensified by the nature of their pupils,
but again this had little to do with pregnancy. Most of the
Project girls had stayed back in school at least one year and
were usually working behind their age and grade levels. The
teachers, and frequently the girls as well, viewed the small
Project school as a chance to make up past school deficien-
cies.

The teachers were not involved in out-of-class Project
activities. They did not attend the group discussion meetings
run weekly at the school by the social worker and nurse, nor
did they attend the evening meetings of the girls' mothers
except when specifically requested to talk about the school.
And finally, the teachers were not briefed about the lives and
problems of specific girls, nor generally about the orientations and intentions underlying the mental health aspects of
the Project.

Their noninvolvement in any but the strictly educational
aspects of the Project can be understood in two ways. First,
the teachers were essentially on loan from the Board of Education and their primary commitments and responsibilities
remained with that organization. Second, the teachers were

not required by the nature of their jobs, as were the social worker and psychiatric nurse, to form a set of coherent notions about the sexual behavior of teen-agers, pregnancy, and dealing with unwed mothers.

This is not to say that the teachers did not have or express opinions on what is appropriate behavior for teen-age girls, but these remarks were casual, unofficial, and out-of-class. And it is precisely because the teachers were not involved in the official mental health orientations of the Project that these casual and direct remarks frequently countered the more subtle goals of the social worker and nurse.

Dealing with the girls' immediate and longer-term out-of-school lives thus fell to the social worker, Mrs. Eckerd, and to the psychiatric nurse, Mrs. Ames.

The social worker bore chief responsibility for formulating and expressing the Project's orientations and objectives to the girls. She had been involved with the Project from the days of its original planning and handled the initial interviews with girls and their families. In contrast, the nurse's affiliation with the Project was part-time and not long-term. Her work there was part of her training as a psychiatric nurse and was undertaken to fulfill the requirements of an M.A. degree. The social worker essentially acted as her supervisor.

Mrs. Eckerd and Mrs. Ames each ran a weekly group discussion meeting at the school during the school day. These meetings, which will be referred to as the group meeting (with the social worker) and the health meeting (with the nurse), were the major context in which girls were faced with the mental health aspects of the Project. For the girls, these discussions represented the primary distinction between this school and schools in general.

The social worker approached these meetings with a conception of what the group discussion might accomplish, a conception of how a group discussion should operate, and a conception of how she should act in running the discussion.

The ideal group meeting from the social worker's point of

view would be one in which girls discussed the questions and problems that bothered them; the discussion would ideally be directed toward the expression of feeling rather than toward the direct acquisition of knowledge. Her comments, both during the meetings and in her own written records of discussions, conveyed her views of what questions and problems might be most usefully discussed and of what feelings ideally would accompany the discussion.

Mrs. Eckerd explained the group for the benefit of several newcomers, "Frequently girls at this age may have problems with mother. Sometimes they have problems because of their boyfriends. This group is to talk about things that may bother you—about the baby, about sexual relations."

* * *

During a burst of conversation about whether it was possible to get pregnant without intercourse (arising from a tabloid story), Mrs. Eckerd said, amidst the din, "I think that in a group like this we could spend all of our time talking about these stories, but I think the group is best suited for talking about things close to you, problems you are involved in."

The discussion ought to be serious, involving everyone. Breaking in on a heated argument over birth control, Mrs. Eckerd comments:

"I think of this as the kind of group where everyone has a chance to say what they think—even the girls with soft voices. The girls with loud voices should allow the others to say things too. I think Belinda has brought up a real problem which can be talked about. The last time this subject came up there was so much giggling about it that we had to stop talking about it. I think this is the kind of thing we should talk very seriously about. . . . Are you interested in continuing to talk about this?"

Several girls nodded, and Mrs. Eckerd concluded, "Well we will talk about it next week but I want each of you during the week to think about it very carefully."

In her abstract of a similar discussion several months before, the social worker writes:

> There was considerable giggling and pairing off. I said that birth control as a matter of information should be discussed by both girls and mothers, in their separate groups; however, I felt their behavior indicated that they were not ready for a serious discussion. When they felt ready, their wishes should be told to the leader.

The social worker hoped to foster this kind of ideal discussion by providing support so that feelings which seemed unworthy, disrespectful, or for other reasons were kept under cover would emerge. She viewed herself as encouraging girls to express themselves and to alter and operate responsibly in their environment. In this way, she hoped to help girls develop abstract skills which could be carried outside the group: seeking information from valid sources, accepting responsibility for the results of one's behavior, taking responsibility for the course of one's life, and communicating one's problems with adults interested in helping.

In a written abstract of a meeting with a group of girls who had left the Project and returned to their regular schools, the social worker comments:

> There was considerable discussion about how to avoid intercourse and the use of birth control methods. I was impressed with the ability of the girls to accept responsibility for their behavior and to discuss experiences where they had successfully avoided intimacy by self-control and action which reduced sexual stimulation. I interpreted their discussion as meaning

that a girl could help herself, either by new knowledge or skill in handling dating situations.

Her stance, that of a professionally trained social worker, was reflective and morally neutral. While she had both professional theories and personal opinions about sexual relations and pregnancy, neither were expressed in the group meeting. Sometimes the style of moral neutrality merely serves to give moral messages more subtle guises, as, for example, when psychological analyses are used simply as a form of moral persuasion. Yet it was the style itself, expressed straightforwardly and without a hidden agenda, that had consequences on the Project. It was simultaneously unbelievable, unbelieved, misunderstood, and unacceptable to the Project girls.

THE GIRLS' VIEWS OF THE PROJECT

Girls came to the Project in order to go to school; they came more and less voluntarily and with greater and lesser interest in education per se, but they understood the school to be the legitimate reason for their involvement with the Project.

My mother ask me did I want to go there or stay home. I told her I didn't *want* to go to this school, but I wanted to make up my grades so that when I have the baby I didn't have to make up eighth grade all over again.

❊   ❊   ❊

I was reading the newspaper and there was Mrs. Eckerd's ugly face. I talked to my mother about it. . . . I was just sitting looking at TV all day long. I didn't know there were schools for unwed mothers. I thought all my friends would be a grade ahead and what would I tell them.

*   *   *

The man at school asked if I wanted to finish school. I said yes and he called Mrs. Eckerd and we came over here and that's how I got here.

It was during the intake interview that girls first became aware of the mental health aspects of the Project—or, to phrase it in the girls' terms, that these people were interested in "your personal business." For many of the Project girls the experience of being asked to offer personal information for reasons they did not understand simply recalled previous experiences with adults in positions of authority.

Dorene said to Mrs. Eckerd, "Mrs. Eckerd, why do adults always be wanting to ask you such personal questions, but you can't ask them the same questions?" There was murmured agreement from the other girls to this.

Mrs. Eckerd replied, "I suppose it depends on what adults you are talking about. Do you mean teachers, your parents—different people have different reasons for asking you different things—"

Dorene said, "I mean why do social workers want to ask you all kinds of personal questions, but you can never ask them back?"

"Yeah, over at the hospital, this lady ask me all kinds of things. Like where was I lying when I got pregnant, was it night or day, how many times did I do it before and do I do it now. Now why do they have to know things like that?"

"What do they want to know that for?" someone else added.

Bernice said, "Yeah, I wonder that, too. Like when my mother and I and my boyfriend went to court, the what-you-call-it prosecuting something or other or somebody was asking all these questions. Now all they asked my boyfriend was two things: did he have relationships with me, and did he make me. And that was all for him. But me they asked everything."

"Yeah, that's what they kept asking me—did he make me, was I sure, did he offer me money, why did I do it. I kept telling them 'No he didn't make me' " Rowena added.

Bernice continued, "They ask you all these questions right there in front of everyone, and all they ask him was two little questions. You're standing up there and this man is asking you, 'Did you do it before?' 'How many times before had you had relationships?', 'Did he force you?' Now Mrs. Eckerd, why do they want to know all that? It's embarrassing."

Mrs. Eckerd said, "I think many times they ask you the questions that they need to know to help you. According to the law a girl under the age of fifteen cannot give consent to have sexual relationships. I think you should ask why they are asking the questions—it's something you should think about and that you should be able to ask other people. You should ask why they want to know."

*   *   *

[How did the people at school find out?]

At first I told the truant officer I had an infected kidney and that was why I would be missing school. Then I quit going regularly to school and I be missing gym. So I had to tell him. He asked me all kinds of questions—had I been picked up for curfew, had I ever been in jail, the boy's name, age, where I lived, did I work after school. He say he didn't know if they would let me stay there or throw me out.

[How did you feel?]

He just be screaming at you like you was some slut dog.

MAY

In fact, Mrs. Eckerd did not herself make these particular sorts of genuinely insulting remarks. Yet there were several features of the intake interview which were distasteful to the girls and which disposed them to take her questions more personally than they were intended.

The social worker viewed the intake interview as a time in which to orient the girl and her mother to the various features of the Project, to array before them such alternatives as adoption and foster home placement, and to make some assessment of the girl and her home situation. Her procedure was to see the mother first, then the girl, then the two together. This procedure made sense in terms of the girls' ages, and in terms of the psychiatric canon that persons speak more freely alone.

Girls, however, resented this procedure, not only because they understood the implied division between themselves and their mothers, but also because the arrangement and the questions created that division. They regarded their talk with the social worker less as an opportunity for unburdening certain feelings than as an invitation to disloyalty.

Someone said, "Mrs. Eckerd talks too much."

Barbara agreed, and said, "Did she ask you all kinds of questions? She asked me personal questions like 'Does your mother treat you nice?' She gives me everything I want. I didn't like the questions."

Bernice said, "Yes, she put my mother in one room and me in another while she asked my mother questions."

I said, "Did your mother tell you what she said?"

Bernice replied, "No. She wouldn't tell me."

Second, even what might be considered the less personal of the social worker's tasks in the intake interview created negative feelings. The social worker regarded it as her responsibility to point out the possibility of adoption or foster home placement; yet girls, and sometimes their mothers as well, experienced this as a moral affront.

She talked to my mother first—asked her did she want me to give the baby up for adoption. My mother say 'No, May be a nice mother.' Yes, she love that child and she feel about it like it was hers. She was mad about it at first.

MAY

*　*　*

She talk to your mother and then calls you in. She tell me about putting my baby up for adoption. I got mad. Later I saw she was right. . . .

[You mean you changed your mind about giving up the baby?]

No. I keep that baby. She was right. Most of the girls get mad but I don't because she's sposed to tell you all she can. I didn't change my mind, I just seen her point.

ROWENA

I myself never attended an intake interview and cannot therefore report what happened there. Yet there is evidence that my presence would have in no way clarified this account, for it is very clear that the intake interview generated a mood in which girls refused to understand what the social worker had in mind and seized upon the ambiguities of conversation to substantiate a sense of unwarranted intrusion. Mrs. Eckerd asked the sorts of questions which are used, particularly by those accustomed to interviewing, to extend a conversation—vague and general questions like "How did you feel?" These are questions which can be misunderstood.

Mrs. Eckerd just jabber-jabber. I don't know what she told me. "How did I get pregnant?" I say, "Shouldn't you know?" She ask some of the stupidest things.

MAY

Yet to a certain extent these were deliberate misunderstandings, as can be demonstrated by the following episode and its denouement. The episode, a parodied intake interview, occurred as girls, gathered for the group meeting, awaited the arrival of the social worker. The denouement occurred in the conversation following her arrival.

The girls became aware of the ticking timer and how late Mrs. Eckerd was, and started speculating where she could be. Somebody said something about her going to the doctor and various girls added:

"To see if she's pregnant."

"She probably thinks that's where you get babies."

"Maybe the doctor's going to give her a baby." This was said suggestively.

Bernice then started doing an imitation interview pretending she was a social worker asking questions of a pretend-pregnant Mrs. Eckerd, "Tell me, how did it feel? Did you like it?"

This brought a storm of laughter, and everybody started mimicking questions they supposedly had had put to them. Someone said, "She asked me did I want to put my baby for adoption, and how did it feel?" She then asked one of the new girls, "Is that what she asked you?"

❋   ❋   ❋

May said to the social worker, "Why do social workers ask so many questions?"

Mrs. Eckerd said, "What kind of questions do you mean, May?"

Bernice, harking back to the earlier conversation before Mrs. Eckerd's arrival, said, "Like 'How did it feel?' " There was an uproar over this, and gradually Mrs. Eckerd got control of the conversation. She seemed angrier than I have seen her and made a determined effort to speak over

Bernice. She finally was able to say, "What do you think I meant?"

Bernice, backing down a little, said, "How I felt about it—if it was right or wrong?"

Mrs. Eckerd said, "Yes. If you think I asked you that, then we should get it cleared up because you certainly misunderstood me."

While perhaps foreshadowed in the intake interview, the girls' dissatisfaction with what I have called the mental health aspects of the Project focused particularly on the group meeting and the social worker, and was expressed in the sentiment that she asked too personal questions.

It is not altogether evident on the face of it what the Project girls meant by "too personal questions." For one thing, much the same topics were discussed in the health meeting in much the same way—yet the girls liked the health meeting. For another, the teachers made much more personal remarks than did the social worker; the teachers were fond, for example, of recommending the "birth control No" as a guide to future behavior, while the social worker avoided expressing an opinion, particularly of that sort.

What girls meant by *personal questions* did not have so much to do with content as it did with the norms of questioning, with their view of the appropriate relationship between themselves and adults, and with their views of the social-work enterprise.

For the Project girls, questions, particularly being asked questions, were an especially salient form of interaction. Questions were experienced as intrusions, as implying *rights to know*, and these rights were allowed only carefully. The right to question belonged in decreasing order to friends, to relatives, to peers, to adults.

Newcomers to the Project school underwent extensive questioning as a kind of ritual preceding inclusion; the questions ranged from "How old are you?" "How old is your boyfriend?" "Where did you go to school?" to "How much do you weigh?" asked of one large newcomer. No one ever objected that this questioning was "personal" and, as far as I could observe, no one refused to answer; yet there was strenuous and united objection to one newcomer who asked similar questions of the others.

Rowena said, "That girl Carla, she ask you the most personal questions. She came up to me—I didn't even know who she was—and was saying, 'When is it due?' and all. I just look at her like 'Who are you?' "

Bernice added, "Yeah, that girl—pardon me, Prue—is full of shit."

Since, in a sense, I spent time on the Project in order to ask questions, at least to have some questions answered, I experienced the Project girls' reservations about questions rather directly. I was only allowed to ask questions after some time, most extensively by girls who had asked me questions[2] and who came to regard me as a friend. The following conversation, which occurred after I had spent about two months at the school, is illustrative.

I asked Rowena privately, "I wanted to ask your opinion about something. Do you think that if I asked the other girls if I could talk to them—interview them, ask them

2. During the first half day I spent at the Project, my presence was totally ignored even during lunch when I sat with the girls rather than with the teachers. The mark of my eventual and gradual inclusion came when girls began to ask me questions; they were concerned first with my age. Later, among the girls who regarded me as a friend, the questions which consolidated friendship included whether I had had sex before marriage. My willingness to answer questions seemed more important than the questions for after these initial *tests*, even friends no longer asked me anything about my own life but simply included me in theirs insofar as that was possible.

questions—do you think they would mind? I thought you would know because you know them better than I do."

Rowena said, "Well I think it depends on the girl. Now you know with Belinda and me you can ask us anything because we ask you anything. But some of the others like Johanna, I don't know. You ask Johanna a question, she's liable to say 'It's none of your business.' . . . Well, like I say, I talk to you because you're a friend. I don't even really know what you do."

For the rest, I was allowed to listen and participate casually in conversation precisely because I did *not* ask questions, and because my age, appearance, and activities marked me as only a quasi adult.

Mrs. Eckerd asked, "Oh, what have you been talking about?"

"We been talking about things just between us, things we can't talk about around you," Bernice answered.

Mrs. Eckerd said, "Why not around me?"

Bernice said, "There are just some things you can talk about around adults and some things you can't. We don't mind Prue being here because she just listens. . . .

Eleanor interrupted, ". . . and laughs when we say stupid things."

The right to ask questions was most severely restricted with respect to adults and had to do with several difficulties and expectations girls experienced in conversations with adults.

First, adults ask questions which are an invasion of privacy, while themselves protected from similar (or any) questions in return. The Project girls did not regard adults in official positions as having a legitimate or helpful concern with their lives; their distrust and resentment was, in large measure, justified by their experience. Furthermore, their wariness in answering the questions of adults in official positions was enhanced by their feeling and experience that what you say to adults counts. The Project girls therefore approached the questions of adults not with trust and candor, but with an eye for the minimal right response. Rowena's account of her court experiences illustrates.

> They took me in the office alone. I was talking to the chief of police. He asked the *same* questions (as the policemen had before): Did I feel he was making me do it, even if he wasn't actually. He say I was young and was I thinking about it. Oh, I was acting real nice and answered every question real polite. They were not going to put me away!
>
> [At her boyfriend's trial] I went before the grand jury, and he did, and my mother—all of us separately. It was continued to the next day. They asked the same questions.
>
> Then we had to go to court for me, because he didn't rape me. If he'd raped me, I wouldn't have to go to court. The judge told me . . . that I be on probation. . . . He introduced me to my probation officer, Miss Firman. I had to talk to her. It was the same questions all over again. After about a month I had to go back to court and she gives a report on me. She gave a real good report. . . . I kept on probation and I been on ever since. They keep records. Now I got a new probation officer. They ask me the same questions usually: how you feel about school, how you feel about your boyfriend being in jail, mostly how you feel about different things. They keep records.
>
> ROWENA

While girls may find it necessary to answer the questions of adults on some occasions, these experiences do not foster a view of adults as disinterested helpers. There were a number of things that the Project girls felt adults had no essential right to know, and questions directed at these matters were felt to be doubly intrusive.

Second, in addition to feeling that there are things they

would not voluntarily discuss with adults, the Project girls felt that there were matters which *could not* reasonably be discussed with adults. Adults are known to represent a particular official moral view on the appropriate activities of teen-agers. Even the most liberal of adults is not likely to recommend, or even to endorse, sexual intercourse to thirteen- and fourteen-year-olds; at best, adults may understand what the odds are, and look the other way.[3] The Project girls in fact shared the ideal moral views of adults but felt that the specific day-to-day problems of relations with boys could not be reasonably discussed with adults, particularly *responsible* adults in official positions.

Third, it can be said that the Project girls regarded representing the ideal moral view as the appropriate business of adults. In this sense, some matters *should* not be discussed with adults, if only as a matter of respect for adults and their expected function. The Project girls were, for example, outraged at the candid remarks of Belinda about birth control and sexual relations in group meeting; the following comments are made by Belinda's best friend, and therefore represent the most tolerant view of what she said.

> "Yeah—shooooo. You shouldn't say what she says. Like that time she was saying about them getting hot and wanting to have intercourse. It's probably true, I don't say it isn't, but she should say it some other way. More deli-

3. Given the extent of sexual activity in Negro lower-class life (see Hammond and Ladner, 1969), this particular relation between girls and adults, particularly their relatives, did not really serve to disguise sexual activity, as is the case among middle-class girls who are also inclined not to discuss their activities with adults. Instead, there seemed to be a tacit agreement between girls and adults not to force certain issues which for the adults would serve to underline their lack of control over children, and for girls would dramatize the discrepancy between ideal ways of acting and the actual pressures and incentives to act otherwise.

cate. And lots of girls talk about how they feel. I've heard the others say how they feel about it with a boy. But they don't want to talk about that in front of Mrs. Eckerd."

I said, "Why not? Because she's older?"

Rowena said, "Yeah, well she's older. And I don't know —she has an education and a career, and she's married and doesn't have any kids. It just seems like you've got to respect her. And it just doesn't seem right to talk about some things around her. She's different from us. She's an adult, and we know we're not."

For their part, adults are expected to express their opinions and to give information. From the social worker's notes:

Johanna said it would be important for the leader to join in the discussion. Her caseworker at Family Service Bureau had just "sat back and let her do all the talking." She felt that she learned more by listening to the "ideas of grownups."

Ann talked about how difficult it was to talk with her mother, and she thought it would be easier to talk with an "outsider." Terri had a different opinion; she felt adults could not understand adolescents. Ann wanted the leader to give specific answers to questions asked by the girls. Elaine said she had belonged to a "Y" club and she thought she understood; she explained how the club had conducted a discussion session on sex. Dora said she was not too clear about how discussion could be handled with adolescents: "Who would decide what was right?"

The Project girls' responses to the mental health aspects of the Project must be understood in terms of these sentiments about the questions of adults, and their expectation that adults will and should express opinions.

The girls had a high regard for the health meeting run by the psychiatric nurse for she tended to answer questions rather than asking them and was the official dealer in information, particularly about pregnancy and birth which were matters of some anxiety to girls. Much of what went on in the health meeting, in fact, had more to do with feelings than information. On the one hand, many of the questions asked were basically unanswerable, for example: "What if you're not near the hospital when your baby starts to come—what if you're in a forest preserve or something like that and there are no people around?" On the other hand, much of the information was ambiguous and obscured by the emphasis on participation and group discussion. For example, the girls spent one meeting looking at the oversize, spiral-bound pictures of cross sections of the female reproductive system from various angles and at various stages of pregnancy; the following is my comment on the session.

> I found the first few pictures ambiguous; I couldn't tell what angle they were taken from. Mrs. Ames would have Pamela, then later Johanna, read the description from the back of the chart. Since the girls do not read well, and the words were large, the sense of the words was lost and frequently they couldn't be heard or understood. Mainly what the girls seemed to get out of it was an idea of what a baby looked like at various months (they would pick out their own stage) and where the cord, afterbirth, and birth canal were.

Nevertheless, the health meeting could be understood in terms which were not only acceptable to girls but also understandable.

By contrast, the purposes of the group meeting and the social worker were not only occasionally offensive (the questions of an adult) but also opaque. The girls recruited to the Project, particularly the younger ones, have not experienced the style of discussion which was expected of them in the group meeting and did not understand how to go about it.

The most dramatic instance of this occurred toward the end of several months of observation, at the time the Project was being expanded to include high-school girls. At the second meeting of this new group of older girls, the social worker was detained, and the girls ran the first half of the meeting themselves. They had elected officers in the first meeting, and had apparently, with Mrs. Eckerd's help, arrived at a list of topics around which their future discussions would center. There were such topics as: How did I feel when I got pregnant?, How did our mothers feel?, What do we see our futures as being like?, and so on. The elected president opened and ran the second meeting in impeccable parliamentary form. She took the list of those in the group and, beginning in alphabetical order, called the name of the first girl, to whom she addressed all the listed questions; then she called on the next girl, and so on until Mrs. Eckerd arrived and struggled to restore a more casual format.

And this was among the older girls who seemed, on brief observation, much more willing than the younger girls to deal with the *kinds* of questions felt to be important by the social worker.

The younger girls judged the style of the group meeting to be useless in the emphasis on feelings and frustrating because of the social worker's tendency to foster group participation rather than to express her own opinions.

[What do you think of group meetings?]

It's all right if she ever find anything to talk about. Don't talk about anything interesting, just how you feel about this, how you feel about that. I like to talk but not about that stuff. I be about to go to sleep.

[Isn't that true in the health meetings too?]

I like how she talks. She explains what you have to go through, how you're going to react. Like not to be going out and playing football. She finds things interesting to talk about.

MAY

❖ ❖ ❖

Mrs. Eckerd brought up the purpose of the group again, getting no related response. At one point, Johanna said,

"You once said we should wait until the others got back before we talked about some things. But if we wait till everyone is here, including after the new girls have their babies and get back, it will be after school is over."

＊　＊　＊

[How do you feel about group meeting?]

I don't like group meetings with Mrs. Eckerd, but Mrs. Ames is nice.

[Why not Mrs. Eckerd?]

She never answer your question right. And she ask too much of your personal business.

[How do you mean she never answers your question right?]

Like if you ask when you have your baby, how long do your period stay off, she go around the table and ask how about you, and they say everything altogether (talk all at once). And when they get stilled down again, she forget about it.

SELENA

Furthermore there is some question, in matters which were less strictly informational, as to whether the stance of moral neutrality is possible, let alone believable.

Premarital sexual relations (particularly for young girls) was not an area in which girls could expect adults to be neutral, and, viewing the social worker as an adult, they tended to convert her questions into the opinions they expected she held.

Johanna said, "Most girls get mad at Mrs. Eckerd asking questions. But the way I feel, you go home, your mother will tell you the same thing."

The stance of moral neutrality was in fact impossible for the social worker to maintain in the face of the Project girls' ability to find opinion in silence as well as in talk. For, on the one hand, it was not sufficient for the social worker to claim that each girl's decision was her own and should be made in terms of what she felt to be right and appropriate for herself. The girls only and rightly understood this as a way of saying that they, after all, know what is right.

If, on the other hand, the social worker was less passive and explored the possibilities (for example, birth control), she risked insulting girls with unacceptable public versions of themselves. For, as will be seen in the coming chapter, the Project girls were learning in their daily experiences with friends, peers, relatives, and adults more amiable versions of their situation and themselves.

The encounter between girls and the more long-term mental health aspects of the Project as these were represented by the social worker can only be described as a stalemate. It was a stalemate contributed to by the organization of the Project, which separated the school and teachers from other aspects of the Project; by the social worker's conception of her role; and by the girls' expectations of adults.

As a school, the Project made it possible for girls to reassume some aspects of their ordinary round of life. The definition of the girls' larger situation was, however, left for the girls themselves to work out in their everyday experience with friends, relatives, and ordinary adults. For while the Project staff may have had professionally based conceptions of pregnancy and unwed mothers, these were not directly encountered by their clients.

6

The Moral Career of the Negro Unwed Mother

The great discovery that lower-class people make, which middle-class and working-class people find so hard to understand, is that it is possible to live a life that departs very significantly from the way you think life ought to be lived without ceasing to exist, without feeling totally degraded, without giving up all self-esteem.

LEE RAINWATER
"The Problem of Lower
Class Culture" (1966: 28)

It has been common until recently to view the greater levels of sexual permissiveness among lower-class Negroes as expressive of values which differ substantially from those of the larger society. It was in criticism of this view that I described the Project girls' "choice" of illegitimacy and paralleled their initial concerns on becoming pregnant with those of the girls who came to Kelman Place and Hawthorne House.

However, it is also clear that both sexual involvement and pregnancy present different problems for lower-class Negro girls than for middle-class or white girls.

The problem for middle-class girls in their relations with boys is to reconcile growing intimacy and sexual involvement with the demands of reputation and self-respect. The prob-

148

lem for lower-class Negro girls in their relations with boys is to find intimacy and the possibility of a long-term relationship in what is more likely to be a transitory sexual involvement with exploitative possibilities for both partners.

Generally more exposed to sexual conversation and activity, less able to control sexual advances, and less in the control of their parents, the Project girls lacked many of the external constraints on sexual activity which exist for middle-class girls. Also, the Project girls had additional incentives for sexual involvement which middle-class girls do not. Their relations with boys provided them with a variety of things they would not otherwise have, things which for teen-age girls are the source of self-esteem and esteem in the eyes of others—nice clothes, places to go, and other paraphernalia of teen-age life.[1]

Furthermore, the respectability concerns of the Project girls were not so strictly tied to sexual behavior but included such nonsexual and problematic matters as dress, staying in school, and staying out of legal trouble. And in sexual matters, their concerns had less to do with the question of sexual intercourse per se than with the age and financial status of their boyfriends, having a regular boyfriend, the circumstances in which sexual relations occur, and the extent to which they could avoid being exploited or publicly put down.

Because the Project girls were young, and therefore especially aware of the ideal standards for sexual behavior, they were not inclined to publicize their actual sexual involvement, particularly to adults. Yet, for the reasons given, sexual

1. The observations I make here about the Project girls are supported by the more extensive observations made by Lee Rainwater and his students of the Pruitt-Igoe housing project in St. Louis. These studies are reported in Boone Hammond (1965), Hammond and Ladner (1969), Joyce Ladner (1966), and Rainwater (1966, 1969, 1970). I am indebted to their observations and analysis throughout this chapter.

involvement did not require the extensive evasions of intent that I have suggested are characteristic of the sexual careers of middle-class girls. For middle-class girls, pregnancy jeopardizes an internal and somewhat falsely maintained sense of virtue by making the past evident. For the Project girls, pregnancy jeopardized external reputation and, most importantly, jeopardized privacy.

Because the Project girls continued to live at home during pregnancy and kept their babies, they had limited options for secrecy and were open to comment on their past behavior, current situation, and future possibilities. Girls felt themselves to be additionally open to public comment because of their age—even a *married,* pregnant, fourteen-year-old would occasion some speculation.

In some of this public response, girls did experience an assault on their moral status—sometimes directly, as when Marianne's aunt called her a tramp, and sometimes less directly. For example, Rowena's court experiences, designed for her legal protection under the statutory rape code, largely served to remind her that she was now questionable and to ratify in public that she gave consent to sexual relations—a consent illegal for someone her age.

The Project girls were also open to a variety of ambiguous public encounters—encounters which were interpreted and misinterpreted by girls in line with their own fears and sense of embarrassment or shame.

> When I went to buy maternity clothes, I wouldn't let the saleslady know it was for me. My mother and me went to a big store and we went to the maternity clothes, and the saleslady say "Is this for you?" I say, "No." And she say, "I thought you look too young." So then I know how people think. Some people think it's a sin.
> [What did your mother do when you said that?]
> She said, "What you talking about?" and I sort of

hunched and she said, "Oh." She still didn't understand till we went to the dressing room and she asked me why I said that. I said I didn't want people to know I was pregnant. And she said, "Oh, girl." [The tone she imitated was sad and understanding.]

JOALANA

* * *

Bernice said, "Yesterday I rode home on the bus with Laverna and that other girl—Carla. And she kept talking about being pregnant, only she said 'pertinent'—pertinent this, and pertinent that, and kept talking about when are you due, and what you going to do with your baby, and saying how she's going to put her baby up for adoption."

Eleanor said, "She say she going to put her baby up for adoption because her mother didn't like her. And that's her second one; she just say she going to keep on doing that."

Bernice continued, "She was talking so loud on this bus. Me and Carla were sitting there just as quiet as anything. We didn't want all them people on the bus to know we was pregnant, and here's Laverna chattering away—'are you pertinent this, pertinent that.' You see, I had on my black coat and one of the coat buttons was gone so when I sat down it popped open and I had to hold it shut. So she pointed at it and said how I was showing the baby and all. I could have killed that girl. We kept trying to hush her and all she kept saying was, 'I don't care if these people know. Who are they?' "

Rowena said, "If it'd been me, I'd have laid that girl out —right there. Don't mess with me like that. No fooling. I wish it'd been me. She wouldn't talk like that around me for long."

Bernice said, "It embarrassed me so much that when we got off and they went into the drugstore for something, I just went on by myself. And she was talking about the men we passed and how she'd do it. On that bus we was the regular main attraction. I turned my head away once to shade my eyes from the sun, and saw this man staring at me like he was saying, 'Who are you, girl?'"

*   *   *

At first there was one man who lives on my floor and he look at me funny and whenever I went by he would come outside the door. I ask why he stare and he say, "How do it feel?" I say, "It feel just like a lady, I guess." He say, "You glad?" And he say, "I wish you lots of success."

[What did you think before he said that?]

I used to think he was thinking I was so fast, and how her mama should ship her. I thought that man was thinking bad things, so I stop speaking and start staring. I didn't know what he had running through his mind.

MAY

While these responses of others eventually provided girls with terms for making a publicly supported accommodation to illegitimate pregnancy, the girls' first experience was of being newly open to comment—whether favorable or not. And in this, the concerns of the Project girls, braving out pregnancy in the public eye, differed importantly from the concerns of girls like the Hawthorne House girls whose imagination of public response shaped their moral careers, but remained essentially untested.

A second major difference in the situation of the Project girls had to do with the wider ramifications illegitimate pregnancy had for a more than sexual respectability. While pregnancy for middle-class girls jeopardizes sexual respectability by redefining the past, pregnancy for the Project girls jeopardized a more general respectability in the future, for it threatened to be the first step toward a common social fate. I have already suggested that the "choice" of illegitimacy over marriage and the opportunity to go to the Project school were regarded as hedges against a way of life which includes desertion, more illegitimate children, interrupted education, menial jobs, and welfare. Whether these hopes were more hopeful than predictive, they nevertheless expressed girls' attempts to evade some of the long-range implications of their pregnancies.

It is true, of course, that the future is encumbered in some ways for any girl who has and keeps her illegitimate child. The Project girls, however, became unwed mothers in a social context in which illegitimacy was both common, although undesirable, and connected to a way of life with more disadvantages than just having an illegitimate child. The consequences of this for the Project girls' experiences in coming to terms with their situation were twofold.

On the one hand, the Project girls were faced daily and immediately with the prospect of what they might become, the way of life they might come to lead. It was a prospect made more salient and more likely by pregnancy. For this reason, girls were especially receptive to explanations of their situation which pictured their future more amiably. They were, however, simultaneously aware of the realities, particularly the sexual realities, which threatened any intention of reform and any offer of reprieve which depended on reform.

On the other hand, the Project girls could also learn from the example and comments of others living in a similarly fated community, the set of accommodations and adjustments which make an undesirable way of life nevertheless possible.

For girls on the Project, therefore, coming to terms with their situation involved not only conceptions of sexual respectability, but also a larger conception of life's possibilities for a lower-class Negro girl with an illegitimate child. And it is in the light of this more long-range fate that the terms of reinstatement and accommodation must be understood.

PREGNANCY AS A MISTAKE

In the responses of others, girls encountered two views of their situation which offered moral respite and a defense against some implications of their situation. The first was the view that their pregnancy was a *mistake,* and the second had to do with the distinction between being pregnant and having a baby.

The Project girls encountered the definition of their situation as a mistake regularly in the responses of a variety of persons ranging from their mothers to the teachers at the Project school. I have already observed that the definition of an illegitimate pregnancy as a mistake is generally available to girls who are young, pregnant for the first time, contrite, and willing to disavow the past. Yet the notion of mistake had a different salience for the Project girls than for middle-class girls and was differently related to self-conception.

For middle-class girls, the notion of mistake expresses and renews ambivalence over sexual involvement and points to that ambivalence in the past. In other words, their mistake is now recognized to have been a mistake in the past; it is a way of believing that real commitment to sexual activity had never existed.

For the Project girls, the issue of their past commitment to sexual activity was not at stake; the Project girls were never concerned to discover "why they got pregnant." If they now viewed their situation as a mistake, it was in the sense that they "saw the light of their ways" and had discovered the price of acting non-ideally.

For middle-class girls, the notion of mistake offered the possibility of erasing and redefining some self-implicating features of the past. For the Project girls, the notion of mistake offered the possibility of reform in the future.

As a recommendation for the future, the notion of mistake was, however, ambiguous. For while sexual involvement was generally understood to be the rectifiable mistake, many of the adults who responded to the situation of the Project girls were aware of the pressures, incentives, and conditions of black, lower-class life which foster sexual involvement. And while they might generally feel girls should ideally abstain from sexual relations, they were also aware of the practical difficulties of doing so. When the Project girls encountered the view that their pregnancy was a mistake, they encountered an ambiguous term which could mean one of several things.

[What do you think the teachers and Mrs. Ames think of the girls here?]

To my way of thinking, that they be a little bit too fast, and if their mother was strict, they won't come up pregnant. Another thing they think is that every girl is entitled to one mistake as long as she don't bring two on the house. They are very nice about it.

[What about a girl who gets pregnant a second time?]

That's not no mistake, when you come up with a second baby. You should control yourself, or if you're going to do it, make him use protection. . . . My mother hasn't got to worry. I'm not even thinking about no intercourse with nobody.

MAY

❁   ❁   ❁

[So what did you say when your mother asked if you had your period?]

I told her No. So she said I was probably pregnant. She was talking all this noise about everyone could make one mistake, but when you keep on doing the same thing, they aren't mistakes anymore.

[What did you think she meant?]

I think she meant it can be a mistake the first time, but

if you do the same thing two and three times, it's not a
mistake anymore. She say you might do the same thing
again, but you can prevent it next time.
[You took her to be saying you should be careful?]
That's the way it sounded.

JOALANA

Yet the usefulness of the mistake view as a reprieve from
shame during pregnancy lay in this very ambiguity. For the
term *mistake* camouflaged a variety of points of view as to
how girls should act in the future and why; it was thus a
normalizing and reinstating theme to which everyone could
adhere. And since virtually all of the Project girls ceased
having sexual relations with their boyfriends following the
news of pregnancy, the ambiguity of the mistake theme as
a recommendation for the future was not a problem during
pregnancy.

As girls approached delivery and reentry into their ordinary lives, however, the issue of sexual relations became
more salient, and the ambiguity of the mistake theme more
apparent. In anticipating the future following pregnancy, the
Project girls faced two interrelated questions—the question
of whether or not they would have sexual relations and
whether or not they would anticipate sexual involvement by
taking birth-control pills or shots. These questions forced
girls to confront the grounds on which their pregnancy had
been excused.

FUTURE SEXUAL INVOLVEMENT

Most of the Project girls shared the feelings of adults
around them that premarital sexual intercourse is not ideal,
particularly not for girls their age. For while sexual involvement might at least be understood and excused in an older
girl, it was a good deal less acceptable in a young girl. In this

sense, the Project girls' ages allowed adults to express more ideal expectations for the future than they could have expressed for an older girl. And because the Project girls agreed that girls their age should not have sexual intercourse, they preferred to view sexual involvement as the mistake they had made, a mistake to be rectified in the future. In this, the Project girls' ideal intentions for the future were not unlike those of the girls at the Hawthorne House.

> [Do you think you will have intercourse again?]
> I don't want to have it anymore, but I don't know.
> [What do you think the opinion of the teachers and Mrs. Eckerd is about that?]
> My impression and I think they are right is that at our age we shouldn't be having no intercourse. They only be trying to tell us what's right and wrong.
>
> JESSICA

While the Project girls understood what was ideally expected of them in the future and agreed that sexual involvement was particularly unacceptable for girls their age, they were also aware of the realities which threatened any intention to reform. The Project girls were faced directly and immediately with the example of others, including other ex-Project girls who had become pregnant for the second time. In this sense, girls could not easily take for granted the privileged definition of their own situation as a one-time mistake.

> Several girls were talking, in the school kitchen, about someone they knew getting pregnant again.
> Johanna said, "If I did that my mother would . . . !"
> There was an exchange here about getting pregnant again, and hoping not to.
> Mrs. Knight, a teacher, who had come in during the conversation, announced from over by the stove, "I know a

sure birth-control way not to get pregnant again. It's 100 per cent certain, absolutely 100 per cent."

To these leading hints, the girls were all saying, "What is it?" Mrs. Knight continued, "It's a special form of birth control that's only for unmarried girls. It's especially for unmarried girls, and it's 100 per cent sure." After they asked what it was awhile longer, she said, "You think about it."

Johanna said, "She means don't do it. Don't have no intercourse." She turned back to drying dishes and said in a low voice, "That don't seem to work too well. Don't have no intercourse, but they do."

Furthermore, unlike the girls at Hawthorne House, the Project girls were less inclined to disavow their own past sexual interest. While they might prefer to avoid sexual involvement, even to the point of taking some measures against that possibility, the Project girls were nevertheless aware of their own possible temptations.

[Do you still go out with the father of your baby?]

No. He come see the baby. But I don't go with him anymore. He's all right. He never did anything too much for the baby. He changes jobs a lot. He treated me all right, till he found out I was pregnant.

[How did he treat you then?]

Not any different. We just stopped going together.

[Whose doing was that?]

My doing.

[Why?]

I thought if we kept going together, we'd end up having relations again. I have enough babies. I just stopped it.

[You're going with someone now, aren't you?]

Yes.

[Do you worry you will have relations with him?]

Yes, sometimes. So far, I haven't anything to worry about so far.

JESSICA

❃   ❃   ❃

Talking to Rowena on the way to her house, she mentioned that Mrs. Johnson, one of the teachers, had talked to her. She said, "She say she think I'm going to go far and get whatever it is I want. She say she don't think I will need any birth control. She say she's sure she's not going to see me back again in a year."

I said, "Are you going to use birth control?"

Rowena said, "Yes. I might not need it. I don't intend to have any more sexual relationships but I know me and I know Edgar [her boyfriend]. I know me too well. . . . When he's talking, he make you *want* to do it. And even if he don't, you want it because you've had it before."

And finally the Project girls could not always count on being able to refuse sexual involvement whatever their own wishes might be. During the time I spent on the Project, Rowena was nearly raped in a housing project elevator; Selena maintained she was pregnant by rape. Even without consideration of such extreme examples, the patterning of relations between the sexes, a pattern of competitive and exploitative seduction (Hammond and Ladner, 1969; Rainwater, 1969, 1970), favored a form of seduction milder than rape yet harsher than tender regard.

[What do you think you will do about sexual relations and birth control in the future?]

I don't intend to have any more intercourse, but sometimes a girl goes out and gets in a jam. I prefer to play it safe. Also there's a boy that may ask me to go with him.

[How is that?]

He looks like he will ask me to have intercourse. I tell

him I already had a baby and don't intend to have no intercourses with anybody. I tell him if he wants a sexual dollie, go out and find one. I tell them where we stand. But even if I say No, especially where I come from, I might as well have said Yes.

MARIANNE

Agreeing to ideal versions of their future sexual behavior, the Project girls nevertheless cast a practical eye toward the likelihood of living up to the ideal standards which they held for themselves. And in the structure of this situation there lies an important and general difference in the concerns of the Project and Hawthorne House girls. The Project girls were generally much less likely to assume that they could run their lives ideally.

In the face of ideal standards, the Project girls could not ignore the realities which made those standards unrealistic. Yet in the face of those realities, the Project girls did not wish to abandon all claim or intention to an ideal sexual respectability. Like the Hawthorne House girls, they were not disciplined adherents of premarital sexual freedom; this is evident in the following excerpt from Mrs. Eckerd's account of her meeting with seven girls who had delivered and returned to their regular schools.

"Elaine had not resumed sexual relations because she wanted to 'uplift' herself and make a better life for herself and her baby. She consciously attempted to control sexual urges because she feels such relations should wait for marriage.

"All the other girls had had relations since they delivered. Only two were using the pill. Jane became angry, saying it was 'nobody's business.' She began a tirade about girls who say they are virgins—'All teenagers had sexual relations.' I interrupted to say that what she seemed to be saying was that she did not feel too comfortable about her sexual behavior.

"After a period of silence, Jane said she guessed she felt like a 'bad girl.' She did not want to see herself as bad, and didn't want to admit to herself that she had had sexual relations last weekend. She felt anxious and took excessive precautions against pregnancy. Her boyfriend was anxious too, and they had agreed they would not have intercourse again. Jane asked if it was true that I had not had sexual relations as a teen-ager. My answer was an emphatic Yes, and the group responded to the tone of my voice. Georgene wanted to know how I could want to work with them."

Accustomed to not being able to live up to their own hopes and standards, the Project girls could at least insist on making their accommodations privately. The great store placed by the Project girls on keeping themselves to themselves, expressed in their feelings about being questioned and about the publicity of pregnancy, must be understood as ways of handling the inevitable discrepancy between standards and behavior. It is perhaps ironic that we tend to take a concern for internal standards over against external reputation as the mark of a finer moral sensibility, when we could as easily view it as a luxury afforded those whose reputation is hardly ever in question.

It is in the light of these observations that the following episode and its aftermath can be understood.[2] While many of the Project girls planned to settle for a lesser good—by considering birth control rather than abstinence—most girls kept their plans private, except to close friends. In this way, girls made the necessary accommodations to reality and to

2. It may be worth noting that this episode occurred on the first day I spent on the Project; at that time I took what was said only at face value. In one sense, what I have written about the Project is based on the history of my understandings of this episode, for I came to see what the girls said not only in terms of their sentiments about sexual relations and birth control, but in terms of their sentiments about adults, privacy, and the possibilities of acting ideally.

their hopes for a general respectability without publicly re-linquishing their claim or mild hopes for a more ideal sexual respectability.

There was the usual foot-shuffling silence where every-one looks down or casual. Mrs. Eckerd said that the group was for questions they might have, about problems with mother, with boyfriends, sexual relations, and so forth. Her comments were delivered in dead and somewhat em-barrassed silence. At the end she asked if they wanted to talk about anything in particular.

Belinda, new to the group, said, "You said we would talk about birth control, about ways not to have babies."

From this point on feelings ran extremely high in the group. There was a burst of noise from everyone. Then Johanna took the lead: "Girl, what you want to know about that for? Ain't you learned your lesson?" Everyone laughed.

Belinda, defending herself against clear attack, said, "I just don't want this to happen again. If I do get—have in-course with a boy—then I want to know what to do not to have a baby. I'm not saying I'm going to, but if I do then I want to know."

Darlene exclaimed, in a tone not reproducible in print, "Oooooooo—Oooooo." Each "Ooooo" rises in pitch, and the tone expressed, "What *are* you *saying* girl!"

Johanna, looking eloquently at Darlene and then at Belinda, said, "I can't believe. . . . You mean you going to let a boy. . . . Then you deserve what you get."

At this point feelings were extremely high against Be-linda. Mrs. Eckerd tried to calm everyone down with a short speech on giving one another a chance to talk, treat-ing the subject seriously. The meeting was coming to an end, and the subject was to be postponed to the next week. Before the meeting ended, Johanna and Belinda had one last exchange.

Johanna said, "You say you love that boy?"
Belinda said defensively, "Yes, I do."
Johanna said, "You going to marry him?"
Belinda said, "Yes. I am."

Johanna made an amazed expression, and observed, "You'll end up like those winos on 54th Street," implying that Belinda was hooked on sex.

Belinda retorted, "The Lord drank wine, and he ain't no wino." There was laughter over this. The timer rang and ended the group meeting. There was still a lot of feeling as we went upstairs.

Several months later Rowena referred to this meeting in speaking of her intention to get pills.

If I were to say anything I would say I'm going to take them in *case*. But with Mrs. Eckerd sitting there, I wasn't going to say nothing.

[Why is that?]

She grown. I got more respect than to say I'm going to do it. . . .

[Do you say that about intending to have intercourse again and use birth control in front of other girls?]

I say it in front of them, but not in front of Mrs. Eckerd. They feel the same way. Around each other they don't hide nothing. What set Belinda out was that she was going to say it whether Mrs. Eckerd was there or not. The others be saying something and lying at the same time. I wasn't going to say it, and I wasn't going to lie. I just keep my mouth shut.

ROWENA

*   *   *

[Do you plan to use birth control?]

I don't want to use pills. My mother say something about it every time she comes home from mothers' meeting. I'd rather take shots. She would rather have me take those than the pills.

[How come people don't talk about this in group meetings?]

We talk amongst ourselves more freely than with the grown-ups. So they wouldn't say anything around grown-ups.

[Why is that?]

They always do that. Most of the girls I know—well, Terri and Gini—they are going to take birth-control shots, but around Mrs. Eckerd or Mrs. Ames they say they're not going to take them.

JOELANA

❋　　❋　　❋

[You said you wouldn't tell the other girls here about taking pills—why not?]

I just wouldn't want them to know. I would maybe get to be the talk of the school—I don't know.

MARIANNE

The Project girls found relief from shame during pregnancy in the view of their situation as a mistake, less because the notion of mistake ratified a sense of moral renewal than because the notion of mistake served as a publicly endorsed defense against undue and undesirable public comment.

HAVING A BABY

Like the girls at Hawthorne House, the Project girls found compensation for the demeaning aspects of their situation in the prospect of having a baby. Yet the experience of moral reprieve through motherhood was markedly different for the Project girls, not only because they kept the baby, but because, in the definition of their situation, the notion of motherhood was less salient than the fact of the baby itself.

From the beginning of pregnancy, the Project girls were committed to keeping their babies; despite the efforts of the social worker to describe the options for adoption and foster-home placement, virtually no girl gave these options serious consideration and were in fact offended by the suggestion.

However we may choose to understand it, many more Negroes than whites are inclined to keep an illegitimate child and are much more likely to be advised by others, most importantly their mothers, to do so (Bowerman, Irish, and Pope, 1963–1966: 84, 207). Yet, while these differences between Negroes and whites exist even within the same social class, they must not be overemphasized. Lower-class whites are also more likely to be advised to keep the child than to have it adopted and are more likely actually to keep an illegitimate child than to have it adopted (Bowerman, Irish, and Pope, 1963–1966: 84, 207). It would generally appear that adoption is the more difficult decision to make, requiring not only opportunity but a fairly sophisticated rhetoric for assuring the girl and those close to her that she is not acting immorally or insensitively in giving up her own child.

While keeping an illegitimate child is reputationally and perhaps realistically difficult, placing the child for adoption is likely to be a more fundamentally ambivalent decision. Ambivalent toward adoption, the girl who also is faced with the likelihood that her decision will be viewed as wrong by those closest to her is likely to be forced to agree. It is instructive, in this regard, to describe the situation of one of the few Negro girls at Hawthorne House. Intending to place her baby for adoption, she underwent a total change of mind following delivery; while this change in itself was not rare and might have been predicted on the basis of her personality (the staff view), the particular circumstances in which is occurred indicate the renewed imperative of her background and the opinions of those at home.

Marlene said, "I guess Negroes are like that some. They feel that you ought to keep your own children, and that you wouldn't think of giving them away. It was sort of terrible in the hospital. There was a Negro nurse there who brought my baby to me several times, and every time she came, she would say, 'How can you give up a beautiful baby like this?' She was offering to let me come and live with her, and she would support me and everything. It was really hard to take. She was really upset with me. . . . If I decide to keep Alice, I'd like to go back and tell her."

A few days later, still very ambivalent about adoption, Marlene said, "I know that if tomorrow I say that I've decided to give Alice up because it's the best thing for her, I'll probably be crying, and then after that, I won't go home on Tuesday. I'll hang around somewhere, but I won't go home. I couldn't face my mother. She'd be crying and saying 'I miss the baby,' and all my brothers and sisters would be the same way. I just couldn't face it."

* * *

Sandy, who had been with Marlene in the hospital, had not heard of her final decision to keep the baby. When Louise told her, she said, "Oh, I bet it was that nurse in the hospital that did it. You should have seen her. It was that Negro nurse. Every time she brought Marlene the baby she would say how could Marlene give her up. . . . You remember that one day. She brought the baby a half an hour after she brought all the others. She delayed it on purpose and kept holding it . . . she wouldn't let Marlene hold it until the last five minutes. She just kept saying, 'How can you give up this beautiful baby? Why don't you bring it to my house and I'll take care of it.' "

Sandy told this story not as if she felt this was cruel of the nurse, but as if it were understandable.

Faced with this sort of pressure, many girls might be unable to maintain a decision for adoption, and this pressure is especially likely to exist for the relatively few Negro girls who can and do consider adoption. Without access to opportunities for adoption, Negroes have made accommodations to illegitimacy, accommodations which may now be expressed in their sentiments toward a girl who considers adoption. Marlene was herself illegitimate and therefore could understand, in spite of her own distaste for that fact, that illegitimacy does not make life unviable. While Marlene in a very real sense had a choice, a choice made difficult by her background, the Project girls did not experience themselves as making a choice about the disposition of the child.

The Project girls did not so much *choose* to keep the baby and thereby express the acceptability of illegitimacy but rather *assumed* from the very beginning that they would keep the baby and thus had to be prepared to endure public comment.

The Project girls, however, made a distinction between how they could endure comment during pregnancy and how they could endure it after delivery. Girls who felt ashamed or vulnerable to criticism during pregnancy, to the extent of shrinking from public comment, did not expect to be ashamed or to act diffident about their babies, regardless of how they might feel about the circumstances of conception.

I wouldn't mind friends knowing, but I wouldn't want people that don't be friends to know. I was more ashamed when I was pregnant. I don't try to hide it now.

[You say you were more ashamed when you were pregnant?]

After I had the baby, I wasn't ashamed anymore. I went outside and I find out all my friends are the same way. I take her anyplace now.

JOALANA

*   *   *

[Well, won't they say something when you go back to the school?]

They will probably still say something but probably not as much as they would have been saying at first.

[Do they all know?]

Yes. They probably know about it. They wouldn't say as much after having the baby as much as while I was carrying it.

[Why is that?]

They talk much more while you're pregnant. I never did go anyplace, just across to the store and back.

[Because of that reason?]

Yes.

[Do you still do that?]

I go places now.

JESSICA

This is not to say that girls anticipated no talk after delivery; because many girls withdrew from circulation as much as possible during pregnancy, they were faced with revealing their situation to some through the presence of a baby. To some extent, the Project girls expected that having the baby, especially the actual presence of the baby, would deflect or neutralize criticism by subordinating one set of possible comments to a set of more agreeable and nonthreatening comments about the baby. More importantly, the Project girls expected that their feelings about the baby, and the baby itself, would be a defense against minding comment.

[What will you say when you go back to Detroit with a baby?]

I don't know *what* I do, what I say. I believe I'll say, "She's my little girl, she's my baby," and keep walking.

MARIANNE

* * *

I asked Beverly about friends' reactions to finding out she was pregnant. She said, "The funny thing is that one girl in Los Angeles was spreading the rumor that I was pregnant. She thought it was a lie. I'm just planning to go back there. I'm going there for a week in June, and I'm just going to bring the baby and not say anything. People can say something if they want to. I just won't say anything about it. I'm planning to take it to church with me so they'll all see me there.

* * *

[What's going to happen when you go back to school?]
They going to talk. I guess it would be hard on some people. I love my baby enough that I don't care what they say.

ROWENA

In making a distinction between their situation during pregnancy and their situation following birth, the Project girls were supported, even during pregnancy, by others' interest in the baby. Yet while others' interest in the baby deflected attention from the less wholesome aspects of the girls' situation, it did not provide them with a sense of transformed identity. For, unlike the situation of girls at Hawthorne House and the situation of middle-class women more generally, the situation of the Project girls was defined not in terms of becoming a mother, but in terms of having a baby.

In their reactions to her situation, others were more likely to express a direct interest in the baby and in their own relation to the baby than in the girl herself or in the girl's relationship to her baby.

It is sort of embarrassing. You be embarrassed like that on a bus, but among your friends and family, everyone feels glad toward a newborn baby in the family—especially in my family. There hasn't been a newborn baby in my family for seven years.

Still everybody don't know I'm having a baby. The ones who know treat me real nice. They ask, "Can I be the godmother?," "Can I name it?," "Name it after me." They don't treat me like I did something wrong. They treat me nicer now than before I was pregnant. My girlfriends give me things and say, "You tell your baby this is from me." They just want to name it, just want to play with that baby. They ain't thinking about me.

[Is this just girls, or adults too?]

Adults too. Everybody. They're always saying, "Be careful." I was carrying a case of pop and everybody say, "What you doing carrying that heavy pop for?" I say, "This ain't no heavy pop." My girlfriends say, "I be glad when I can get me a baby." They just like babies.

ROWENA

❖   ❖   ❖

[Have you decided about names for the baby?]

If it's a boy, I was thinking about Demetrius. If it's a girl, Camellia, after my sister.

[Where does Demetrius come from?]

After a girlfriend. Her father wanted a boy so bad, he gave her a boy's name.

[Do you ask your boyfriend about naming the baby?]

I don't ask him. He said once to call it Baggie, and I say I'm not going to name it that. He say he don't care what I name it. He just want to run the street with it, show it to his friends.

MAY

❖   ❖   ❖

[How has the baby affected you?]

Well, now all my goodies go to the baby. All the goodies

go to Sarah now and not to me. My auntie takes me downtown a lot, but my mother hasn't bought me anything.

MARIANNE

The Project girls were not regarded as exclusively responsible for their babies. In one sense, their age made the assumption of full motherly responsibilities difficult, for not only were they still in school but they also were still wrapped up in the usual concerns of young teen-agers—having good times, being free to go places, being on the street.

More generally, however, the Project girls shared a way of life in which motherly responsibilities were usually diffused among a number of persons. The Project girls themselves had been involved in caring for their younger brothers and sisters and were themselves cared for by a variety of aunts, stepfathers and stepmothers, mothers—persons who, for reasons of blood relationship or sense of kinship,[3] took interest in them. The Project girls' babies thus did not so much enter the world to an exclusive relation to a single mother, as to a web of persons with a variety of interests and concerns in their welfare.

In relation to this, Bowerman, Irish, and Pope (1963–1966: 261) observe that "Whereas *two-thirds* of the white respondents granted that the baby belonged to the entire family, *four-fifths* of the Negro subjects stated that view." Although this evidence does not include the less usual situation of middle-class girls who keep an illegitimate child, it

3. The Project girls frequently spoke of their "aunties," and included in this term not only blood relatives but close, older female friends of their mothers who took special interest in them. Elliot Liebow (1967) has remarked at length on the use of kinship as a model for other kinds of relationships among the Negro men he studied. Their aunts seemed to serve the Project girls as adult girl-friends to whom they could confide things they were reluctant to confide in their mothers. Not infrequently, the Project girls' mothers had learned of the pregnancy not from the girl herself, but from one of these other relatives.

would appear that diffusion of responsibility for the baby is one solution to the problems raised for girls who keep an illegitimate child, and is a particularly common pattern among lower-class Negroes for whom illegitimacy is a common fact of life.

While this arrangement allowed girls to resume their usual lives, it also deemphasized their exclusive relationship as mother to the baby, for their motherhood was not the focus of others' concerns and was diffused among a number of persons. If the Project girls found solace from the demeaning aspects of their situation in having a baby, this had less to do with a transformed sense of themselves as mothers in their own and others' eyes than with a transformed sense, however temporary, of life's possibilities. The baby provided them with things to do, plans to make, and some compensation against a sense of deviance, but, most importantly, against a life uneventfully located in the present.

You feel maturer because being a mother is a new thing to you. You feel just like a grown-up. You did everything a grown-up did, and it's bound to make you feel more mature. You know more about life.

In a way it's nice, and in a way you ask why when you be so young. But I'm not the only young child in the world having a child. . . .

Because you're a mother, there are all possibilities to take on. There are things to do now, and it's a nice feeling being able to do things grown-ups do. But I could have at least waited.

MAY

In the process of becoming an unwed mother, girls on the Project and at Hawthorne House were provided with the materials for the evasion of deviant identity. In many respects, the life circumstances of girls on the Project and at Hawthorne House differed dramatically, as did the central features of their solutions to the problem of an illegitimate pregnancy. Yet both groups of girls encountered some version of the notion that their situation was a *mistake,* and both encountered a moral distinction between the treatment accorded pregnant girls and that accorded mother and baby.

Perhaps the most crucial difference in the experience of these two groups of girls was not so much in the responses to their situation, but in the extent to which girls could themselves believe in the moral reprieve offered. The moral career of a girl at Hawthorne House can be described in terms of moral reinstatement for she could believe she had made a mistake and could believe in her own transformation, however temporary, to motherhood.

Not isolated from her ordinary life in a special institution, the Project girl could less easily believe herself changed. For the Project girls, the *mistake* view and the distinction between being pregnant and having a baby were not so much self-believed transformations of self as defenses against a more externally defined deviant identity. And for this reason, the moral career of a girl on the Project was necessarily a more cynical, if more realistic, enterprise—a matter of acting on private reservations while expressing and, to some extent, believing in more publicly acceptable versions of herself.

Speculations:
The Politics of Illegitimacy

In the course of this book I have provided a rather detailed description of the experiences during pregnancy of unwed mothers who spent several months of pregnancy in a maternity home and a maternity school. My description has been organized around the conception of moral career, around the view that illegitimate pregnancy presents girls with a limited set of alternatives and a particular sequence of concerns and experiences of self. The purpose of these final comments then is to mention some of the issues which could not be easily fitted to that descriptive account and to point out the larger contexts in which I regard this study to be embedded.

It has been customary to justify research on unwed mothers on the grounds that illegitimacy is a social problem of some seriousness, one which is increasing numerically and proportionally; and it has been customary to locate the sources of this social problem in an alteration in the sexual values which have supported legitimate family life (for example, Vincent, 1961).

In the first chapter I detailed one of my reservations about this point of view, suggesting that illegitimate pregnancy, at least among white and middle-class girls, might well be regarded as the product of conventional concerns rather than of unconventional commitments or pathological motivations. Even if the question of motivation is set aside, however, it is unclear in what sense illegitimate pregnancy constitutes a social problem.

Abortion and marriage are the most common solutions to the problem of illegitimate pregnancy among white women, and since the current evidence (as reported in Coombs et al., 1970) suggests that 20 to 25 per cent of white brides are pregnant at the time of marriage, it would appear that an illegitimate pregnancy is not an uncommon route to marriage and legitimate family life. Furthermore, it has been estimated (Adams and Gallagher, 1963) that about 70 per cent of white children born illegitimate are placed for adoption. These figures suggest that even illegitimacy, as distinguished from illegitimate pregnancy, if a problem, is for white women a socially invisible one charted largely in the feelings of women who choose to give up an illegitimate child.

This is not to say that illegitimacy is not a social problem of some proportion, but that the shape of that problem is determined not only by the sexual attitudes and behavior of unmarried girls and women but also by the differential availability and use of alternative solutions to the problem of pregnancy. To illustrate, illegitimacy is more common among Negro women not only because premarital sexual experience and therefore pregnancy are more common, but also because abortion is so much less common a solution to the problem of pregnancy.

It is in this sense that the definition of illegitimacy as a social problem, a social problem with sources usually traced to sexual behavior, is something of a political act. For it is a definition which not only tends to deflect attention from social inequalities in access to other solutions to the problem of pregnancy—primarily abortion—but also supplies support for the questionable view that having and keeping an illegitimate child is the least acceptable solution to the problem of pregnancy. That is, when the relationship between illegitimate pregnancy and illegitimacy remains unexamined, we tend not to see the part played by social policies in allocating illegitimacy to one class of women without, however, helping them to live with that solution.

Generally speaking, it is difficult to separate theoretical issues from social ones in the area of illegitimacy, for theory and research on unwed mothers have depended to a large extent on the characteristic services available to unwed mothers. And although both theory and services have been grounded in the view of illegitimacy as a social problem, neither has fit the actual distribution of that problem.

Both in terms of proportion and in terms of proportional increase, illegitimacy is more common among women over twenty than among teen-agers and much more common among Negroes than whites. Yet teen-agers and white women especially are more likely to receive social agency services, largely because agencies offering services to unwed mothers have defined and organized their function around adoption—an alternative primarily available to white women (Adams and Gallagher, 1963; Teele, 1966; Bernstein, 1963). And while many social agencies are currently concerned to extend their services to Negro women, it is unlikely that they will have much success within the conventional framework of child-care agencies and maternity homes, the source of most services to white unwed mothers. To put it a different way, the adoption decision appears to be the most intransigent difference between white and Negro unwed mothers, and the extension of adoption-centered services is accordingly the least useful way to expand services to Negro women.

To summarize for a moment, both the shape of illegitimacy as a social problem and the distribution of services to unwed mothers have been determined to an appreciable extent by the kinds of *escapes from illegitimacy* which have been available to middle-class and white women. Furthermore, perhaps because services for unwed mothers have until recently been predominantly services for temporary unwed mothers—that is, girls who will give up their babies for adoption—the prevailing conception of services for unwed mothers has been directed to the time of pregnancy. Even those services which are now most usefully being extended to the black community—prenatal care and temporary schooling—are services for pregnant girls. Yet for the girl or woman who becomes and remains an unwed mother, the greatest problems exist following delivery when she must arrange both to support and care for her child.

In terms of developing social policies which address the consequences of illegitimate pregnancy, the implications of this analysis are twofold. On the one hand, one of the clearest ways to affect the incidence and distribution of illegitimacy as a social problem is to repeal the abortion laws and to provide abortions free to women who could not otherwise afford it. For unless abortion is legalized, safe abortion will remain an alternative available to those women who possess the right combination of luck, persistence, social contacts, and money—a combination which has worked against poor women, especially Negro women. Abortion is currently a widely used alternative to illegitimacy, but it will only be an equally available and equally safe alternative if legalized.

On the other hand, it is difficult to sustain the position that abortion is ethically or socially preferable to illegitimacy as a solution to the problem of illegitimate pregnancy. In fact, as I have observed, our current, if faltering, social policies ban abortion without, however, providing real social support for the woman who has and keeps an illegitimate child. Even if abortion becomes generally legalized, and especially if it does not, it is therefore necessary to develop social policies which will address the problems of unwed mothers. For unwed mothers, as distinguished from illegitimately pregnant girls, remain essentially without social services.

Unwed mothers are widely held to suffer from their stigmatizing situation, a situation with ramifications for mother and child. It is difficult in the absence of much information about such women's experiences to know how and in what circumstances this stigma is encountered, and even more difficult to imagine social policies for correcting social sentiment. Yet among the most compelling problems which face the girl or woman who, whether by choice or consequence, keeps an illegitimate child are the practical and daily problems of financial support and child care. These are problems which can be addressed.

Currently the only service available to unwed mothers is minimal financial assistance through the Aid to Families with Dependent Children program. For the girl or woman who cannot solve the double problem of support and child care in other, and perhaps undependable, ways, the decision to employ this solution is essentially a decision to become or remain very poor. As Nancy Lee (1969: 153) has cogently observed, "Caring for the child deprives the mother of the opportunity to pursue a job or improve her education and the public welfare or Aid to Dependent Children relief which makes it possible to live and care for the child insures a lower-class standing in the community." In fact, most unwed mothers do not receive Aid to Dependent Children (Adams and Gallagher, 1963), perhaps in part because minimal financial assistance has not offset the liabilities of being consigned to poverty.

Furthermore, while unwed mothers currently lack genuinely adequate financial assistance, on the one hand, they also lack the essential service which might in some measure compensate for lack of real financial support—suitable and relatively inexpensive day-care facilities. Currently the unwed mother who wishes to complete her education or hold a job which provides more adequately than welfare must rely for child care on ad hoc arrangements with family or neighbors or on expensive and transitional baby-sitting arrangements. And it is unlikely that these ad hoc arrangements, subject to change and primarily custodial, are suitable for mother or child.

In this sense, the absence of responsive services for unwed mothers has not only contributed to the set of problems customarily attributed to the inevitable disadvantages of one-parent families but has also undoubtedly supported the unacceptability of illegitimacy and the acceptability of adoption among middle-class girls. For example, while some of the girls I encountered at Hawthorne House seriously considered keeping the baby, they could not construct an acceptable solution to the practical problems they could foresee—prolonged dependence on the financial assistance of their families, welfare, or prolonged dependence on their mothers for child care.

Up to this point I have neglected the issues which are usually raised in connection with illegitimacy—namely, ways to prevent illegitimate pregnancy in the first place, ways to deal usefully with the problems and needs of girls during pregnancy, and ways to extend these useful services to a wider and more representative population of pregnant girls. Because these are issues which have received a good deal of competent and informed attention from others, I have preferred to point to areas which have received less attention.

While I have spoken generally and critically about the structure and viability of the alternatives which face the pregnant girl, it may be useful at this point to mention the specific services which would help to translate alternatives into choices even within the current social framework and which might also address the issues mentioned above.

One of the crucial first steps which mobilizes the illegitimately pregnant girl's concern about the alternatives available to her is medical confirmation of pregnancy. Yet it would appear that many girls do not seek and get medical confirmation of pregnancy early enough in pregnancy to allow themselves time for a reasoned consideration and exploration of the alternatives available to them. For example, a survey conducted by and among the Hawthorne House girls indicated that over fifty per cent had the pregnancy medically confirmed after three months of pregnancy. These girls are, of course, not a representative sample of girls who become pregnant; yet it seems likely that having to reveal the suspected situation, perhaps for the first time, to someone whose reactions cannot be predicted is a source of apprehension, if not delay, for most unmarried girls.

Furthermore, because of the part they play in confirming pregnancy, doctors are currently the initial and central source of pregnancy counseling and referral. Yet the kind of counseling which can be given by doctors is limited, if only because it will be related to the particular doctor's private and professional attitudes toward abortion. More generally, it is currently very unlikely that an unmarried pregnant girl will find her way to an official source of pregnancy counseling which will not only array before her all the alternatives but also support and help her to implement any decision she makes. Specifically, family service agencies are unlikely to support abortion as an alternative; conversely, abortion counseling centers are unlikely to support illegitimacy as an alternative.

In the light of these observations, it would seem that one of the most effective ways of providing services for a wide range of unmarried girls is to create pregnancy counseling centers, staffed with persons who are open and knowledgeable about each alternative solution to the problem of illegitimate pregnancy as well as personally sensitive to the particularities of each girl's situation, and to affiliate these centers with well-advertised pregnancy test services.

The advantages of incorporating pregnancy test services and pregnancy counseling services are threefold. First, the placement of pregnancy test services within a pregnancy counseling center would diminish the apprehension a girl might feel about going either to a family doctor or to a strange doctor and lead to earlier medical confirmation of pregnancy. Second, early medical confirmation would give girls more time for consideration of the alternatives and, since medical confirmation leads naturally to counseling, the affiliation of pregnancy test services and pregnancy counseling centers would sponsor more effective counseling of a greater number of girls.

Third, and perhaps more controversial, the incorporation of pregnancy test services into a pregnancy counseling center opens the possibility for effective and called-for contraceptive counseling for those girls who turn out not to be pregnant but could have been. One of the current difficulties with sex education programs is that practical contraceptive information (which would include ways to acquire contraceptive methods as well as information about how each method works) is a highly explosive subject particularly when offered to presumably sexually inexperienced girls. And yet, as I suggested at length in the first chapter, contraception remains a crucial and yet unexamined, certainly unsanctioned, feature of premarital sexual careers. It is unreasonable, however logical, to suppose that practical contraceptive information can be provided by sex education programs in the current social climate which holds, and rightly, that sanction for contraception is sanction for sexual experience. Yet the provision of contraceptive information and counseling through pregnancy counseling centers particularly to girls who have experienced a pregnancy scare is less likely to be viewed as moral subversion of the young and is a reasonable place to begin, however minimally, to reduce the incidence of illegitimate pregnancy.

Appendix: Methods

A straightforward account of my ways of working is complicated because I essentially did four separate pieces of research—spending time at three settings for unwed mothers and doing an exploratory study of contraceptive use among college girls. While my methods in each case were fluid ones, open-ended interviewing and participant-observation, the particular blend of methods was determined to some extent by the conditions set for my activities in each place. It is perhaps best to begin my account, therefore, with the question of access to maternity homes, for this was importantly related to method.

From the beginning I wished to study not just unwed mothers but unwed mothers in maternity homes. I wanted particularly to study the impact of the theories and practices of maternity homes on their clients, for I imagined that girls' experiences in maternity homes would differ from the experiences of inmates in other sorts of institutions. I felt that my interests would require not only personal conversation with unwed mothers, rather than some less fluid device like a questionnaire, but also involvement in the daily life of a maternity home. In other words, participant-observation.

To maternity homes geared, as they have traditionally

been, to the protection of their clients' identities, this was, however, a particularly demanding request. In one previous study of girls in a maternity home, for example, the researcher, who even had the relevant advantage of being female, was required to interview unwed mothers through a one-way screen (Willy, 1965). I was therefore asking a great deal.

It is not surprising that of the four places I approached, one turned down my request—nominally on the grounds that I would need legal permission for each entering girl from her adoption agency worker—and another, Kelman Place, put severe restrictions on my activities. It is also not surprising, in retrospect, that I was given greatest freedom on the Project, where the question of secrecy was not relevant, and given the least freedom at Kelman Place, the most traditional of the three places I studied.

At Kelman Place I was not allowed to participant-observe on the grounds that some girls might not wish to be seen. My initial contact with the girls there, following several months of negotiation, was with a gathering of girls in the dining room at Kelman Place. I was told that one girl had remained upstairs. I made several visits of this sort but found the formal atmosphere of girls gathered for my visit difficult. I could neither unobtrusively participate in their everyday life, nor did I feel right in asking specific questions of specific girls. Because of this difficult arrangement and because girls expressed their eagerness to be interviewed, I shifted to individual interviewing, seeing two or three girls separately on each visit.

The length of each interview and spread of interviews over weeks, turnover in the home, my lack of access to the group as a whole, and my dependence on the housemother to stir someone up to be interviewed—all combined eventually to give me the feeling of going through some sterile and probably dehumanizing ritual. While both the girls and I enjoyed

the interviews, I felt I was poaching on their troubles with
out finding out what I wanted to know. I spent two months
intermittently interviewing at Kelman Place, but I did not
so much end my research there as abandon it. Nevertheless
I later found these interviews useful in providing systematic
accounts of girls' actions and experiences after suspecting
they were pregnant; and my experience at Kelman Place
provided me with a useful conception of staff concerns in a
traditional maternity home.

At Hawthorne House I was granted my request to participant-observe both among the staff and among the girls, but
I was asked not to interview out of concern for the already
heavy interviewing demands made of their clients. Hawthorne House processes numerous requests for girls' participation in research ranging from medical studies dealing with
girls and their babies to sex education enquiries. Even in the
ordinary career of a girl through the home, a fair amount of
time is spent being interviewed—in the intake interview, in
regular sessions with a caseworker as well as in several interviews with the social worker from the prospective adoption
agency. In addition, a girl may be involved in group therapy.
I think, too, that the staff viewed interviewing, particularly
of unwed mothers, as an essentially psychologically oriented
method and did not wish me to intrude into areas outside my
professional competence for fear of unwittingly upsetting the
girls.

In practice, this condition was not restrictive. On the Project and at Kelman Place I had used interviews largely as a
way of finding out about girls' experiences before coming to
these places. At Hawthorne House, girls spoke freely and
spontaneously about these past experiences in conversations
with each other and in the group-therapy meetings I attended. Formal interviews were therefore not necessary.

On the Project there were no restrictions on my activities
except for those imposed by the situation and the girls. While

this lack of restriction is understandable in view of their clients' inability to maintain secrecy about pregnancy, it was nevertheless generous of the Project staff, for my participant-observation occurred in what was, after all, a grammar-school classroom.

Aware of the conditions made for me in each place, I have come to see that the question of my method had theoretical ramifications of which I was initially unaware. For while my preference for fluid methods, particularly participant-observation, was dictated by my original theoretical concern, my intended method tended to select some settings and not others. The two settings I studied most extensively were those least traditional and most committed to the idea of research. Although I did not intend it—for I was unaware of the varieties of maternity homes and, at any rate, could not have consciously sampled maternity homes to fit my purposes—I wound up studying two homes which in different ways embody the current conceptions of professional social workers and the directions in which settings for unwed mothers are moving. And in this sense, the conditions set on my activities in each place expressed important features' of the staff orientation toward their clients.

ASKING QUESTIONS

Exploring a general concern with the moral career of an unwed mother with several blends of interviewing and participant-observation among several different groups of girls, I had reason to reflect on the nature of these methods in relation to the differences among the girls and settings. For myself, these reflections have been linked to some observations Harold Garfinkel (1967) has made about the sort of enterprise human conversation is generally.

Garfinkel makes an analogy between the work an everyday person does in constructing sense out of his world, particularly as that world is available to him through conversation, and the work a social scientist does to make sense of his data. The analogy is particularly apt for the field researcher or interviewer whose data come by way of open conversation, and who must usually participate in the construction of that conversation. This sense construction work is referred to by Garfinkel as "understanding work," and the method of looking at a conversational event as standing for a general pattern which can be understood through work, he calls the documentary method of interpretation.

The particular feature of understanding work which I wish to comment on concerns what Garfinkel refers to as the retrospective-prospective possibilities of an event. Persons in conversation tolerate a great deal of (necessary) ambiguity and vague talk, making the assumption that what is being talked about will come to make sense. In employing this wait-and-see attitude they come to provisional understandings of what the conversation has been, is, and will be about, but these understandings have less to do with what the conversation was *in fact* about and more to do with a negotiation process by which persons arrive at a retrospective agreement as to what the conversation was about in terms of what it in fact became. For example, to understand what these words I have written mean in this particular case, the reader must wait until I have made some connection to interviewing and participant-observation to "really" understand what it is I had in mind.

The participant-observer is a double participant in conversation—doing the work of an ordinary participant and doing the provisional theoretical work necessary to acquire material which may become relevant. One of the special features of conversation for research purposes is the trained doubt that I understand what I think I understand. So, for example, Rowena (from the Project) once observed that she was "over-sexed"; I took this to mean either that she liked sex but felt she shouldn't, that she liked sex more or more sex than her friends or boyfriend, or that enough sex to get pregnant is "over-sex." At any rate, I thought I had a general idea of what she meant, and mostly by chance, asked why she thought that. She said, "Because I only like to do it with guys over twenty-five," opening up several other possible interpretations. I chose to "understand" this in reference to her boyfriend's age, twenty-six, and to the girls' disapproval of older boyfriends.

It is of course possible to disclaim the work of the researcher in constructing his own data by converting theoretical interests into fixed questions—interviews, questionnaires. But this merely masks from the researcher's eyes the work being done by his subject.

Most questions asked of persons require them to assess the purpose of asking, for many questions and many answers exist within the same set of words. Even a seemingly straightforward question cannot be answered literally. For example, the *correct* answer to "How many children do you have?" may vary, depending on whether the researcher is concerned with natural children (for a study of childbirth), raised children, at-home children, or wards.

In formal conversational circumstances like interviews and questionnaires, it is usually the sequence of questions and kinds of probes (the small questions used to keep people talking) which provide persons with the primary ways of making this assessment. For example, the interviews that I did with the Kelman Place and the Project girls began with the question, "Could you start by telling me what happened from the time you first suspected you were pregnant?" Girls usually gave a brief, three-minute account; as I began to ask about specific points, they learned the sort of account I had in mind, and the original account expanded, usually taking about an hour and a half.

It is interesting and important to notice the extent to

which interviewees cannot *simply* answer a question and the extent to which good research must depend on them *not to*. Occasionally questions are systematically mis-assessed; these are regarded as bad questions to be rewritten, but they are important examples of the extent to which a good question depends on the existence or negotiation of a common understanding, between researcher and subject, of what is being talked about.

Questions, particularly sequences of questions, invariably have implications no matter how they are put. Questions about contraceptive use, for example, became a particular problem to me. To girls who have had sexual relations, neutral and matter-of-fact questions about contraceptive use imply a rational, technical stance toward contraception, *whether or not the researcher wishes to take that stance.* In one of my initial interviews at Kelman Place, I asked toward the end of a two-hour interview, "could you tell me whether you were using any methods to keep from getting pregnant?" The girl exclaimed, "Oh, you sound just like my mother!"

In further interviews, and in using the contraceptive history interview schedule, I took particular pains to qualify the unintended import of the questions, both by carefully writing the questions toward nonuse ("What contraceptive methods, if any, have you or your partner used?") and by training my interviewers to be alert to hesitations and uncertainties. Even so, the contraception interviews with college students had the effect on at least one interviewee *and* one interviewer of making them more *principled deviants—* more committed users of contraceptive methods. One interviewee commented that she had never had a chance to talk about the subject before. And I found myself in the amusing position of being stranded between my theories (that contraception is not for most girls a technical decision) and my convictions (that girls who are having sexual relations should be convinced to use self-provided means of contraception).

People who are asked questions, particularly by social scientists, also read the intentions of the researcher from their own familiarity with theories about their behavior. In several interviews at Kelman Place, I discovered that my interviewees were social science students in college, had read articles and books about unwed mothers, had applied the theories to themselves, and were presenting me their reinterpreted past in the interview. (Sample: "I think I wanted to get pregnant." [Why do you think that?] "Well, I was reading this book. . . .") At Hawthorne House, and even on the Project, girls were sensitive to the explanations of their situation which they found in magazines, newspapers, and the words of professional social scientists—whether social workers, psychologists, or sociologists. This conversion to social scientists' views of their situation in fact became one of the themes of my analysis of Hawthorne House.

As people increasingly hold opinions and theories about their own actions which are reflected in, and reflective of, the theories of social scientists, it becomes all the more important to discover how people understand the questions they are being asked. As David Riesman (1964) has suggested, it may be necessary to reevaluate the usefulness of the *rapport* interview in the face of subjects who are all too willing to make themselves available to the intentions of the researcher. And it may be even more necessary to reevaluate all forms of formal questioning in terms of the part the researcher plays in the construction of a mutually agreed-upon version of events.

If the researcher cannot count on his subjects to understand what he is doing, however, he faces other difficulties. My experience with girls on the Project made me particularly aware of how much I usually and unknowingly counted on girls to understand my intentions. For although the Project girls were unhappily familiar with being questioned by adults in positions of authority, they were not familiar with the notion and conventions of research. This did not matter so much during the time I spent participant-observing but did in the more ritualized setup of interviews.

Some regarded the interview as a favor and went through it giving the minimal response, less out of any particular hostility than out of deference. More often, girls regarded the interview as a detailed and intimate conversation which created the bonds and debts of a special friendship. They answered my questions from their point of view, in exhaustive detail, branching off into a variety of situations and personal relationships which I could barely follow and which I could not relate to my original question or theoretical concerns.

While becoming a friend was natural, useful, indeed necessary, I sometimes felt uncomfortable about trading on friendship with the awareness that I would be moving on, to another interview, eventually to a different place. Also, being a friend meant "passing" as a teen-ager, occasionally a matter of personal discomfort—for example, in the presence of girls and their mothers, some not much older than myself, or in moments of boredom with the usual talk of young teen-agers. More frequently, being a friend made talking with the Project adults difficult. Many of the usual dispensations allowed a researcher were therefore made problematic on the Project.

And it is also true that conversation was more problematic on the Project because of my own initial unfamiliarity with the circumstances of *their* lives. The amount of time I spent listening on the Project, especially at the beginning, was partly a matter of deference to girls' sentiments about questions. Among the very first things I heard on the Project was the agreed-on feeling that the social worker asked "too personal questions." Since I didn't know what that meant, I figured I'd better find out before I asked any.

But it is also true that initially I did not know what questions would make sense, because I could not take for granted the grounds from which even mundane questions are asked. I found I could not assume I understood what they meant—for example, the person a girl called Mother was sometimes her *real* mother, sometimes her main mother, sometimes her *real* but not main mother. The questions I came to ask in conversation grew out of conversation.

In my initial participant-observation at Hawthorne House as well, I preferred situations in which listening was most profitable—usually informal groups of girls. As I became aware of their spontaneously expressed concerns, and as girls became used to my presence, I talked with girls individually and took a more directive part in conversation.

I have spoken of understanding work in relation to methods of formal questioning as a way of pointing to the special burdens these methods place on the subject in bringing his experience to bear on what he understands about the concerns of his questioner.

Participant-observation tends to shift the burden of this work from the person being studied to the researcher, and tends to make more available to the researcher the context within which the subject is making sense of what goes on, including the questions he may be asked.

While participant-observation suited my own predilections for some of the reasons I have described, participant-observation and interviewing were each suited to different kinds of data. My original intention was to spend time participant-observing, then to use my familiarity to construct and administer an interview schedule as a way of systematizing what I had observed. I found instead that interviewing was most suited to personal and past experience, and that much of the material gathered by participant-observation was not amenable to transformation into an interview question—frequently being too obvious to the participants, or too unacceptable to talk about in a formal interview situation. For example, the ethic that everyone has a right to make her own decisions and the sentiment *Who-am-I-to-judge-another?* were frequently espoused in the interview situation by girls who freely made a variety of personal and moral judgments of others in casual conversation. In this sense, participant-observation and interviewing illuminate different aspects of experience, even when the subject matter is the same.

PARTICIPANT-OBSERVING

As a final reflection on my ways of studying the experience of unwed mothers, I wish to describe what seemed to me the special features of participant-observation, and the consequences these had both for my data and my experience in acquiring it.

Material gathered by participant-observation is gathered through the person of the observer and depends a great deal on the flow of events as they develop and pass. It is usually, and most usefully, material about the present, gathered in the present, through the presence of the observer. One of the ever-present decisions for the field worker, particularly in a large institution, is where to be. The decision about where to be is complicated by the flow of events and the necessity to take time out, if only to collect notes and thoughts.

As I look back on my field notes from Hawthorne House, it is interesting to find that my coverage of events roughly paralleled the girls' passage through the House. I initially attended new girls' meetings, prenatal classes, group activities, sat around in the lounges and snack kitchen. As these became repetitive, I spent more time in girls' rooms, while still attending clinics, group-therapy meetings and staff meetings. As I came to know the girls in the therapy group, I followed their experiences in anticipating the due date and decisions about the baby. And toward the end of my own stay, I spent time visiting the hospital and attending the postpartum meetings.

I did not set out to do this and have only become retrospectively aware of the pattern of my activities. One of the special features of participant-observation, of putting oneself into the circumstances of others, is to create in the observer some of the experiences of those being observed. Hawthorne House had much the same logic for me as for its clients. This sense of involvement is increased by the extent of actual involvement which is required for participant-observation.

Under the press of events, participant-observation becomes a more than full-time job; initially it is necessary to spend a great deal of time in simply becoming familiar and acceptable. For example, at Hawthorne House I wished to distinguish myself from the staff members and did this by spending weekends and evenings there. (On the Project I solved the same problem by leaving school when the girls did.) As I became familiar and acceptable, I became involved in following a variety of events, both among the staff and girls. Furthermore, I became missed in absence so that once when I had spent one day with the staff, and a day away, girls wondered where I had been for so long.

On the Project, this was an even greater problem for I had to travel fifty miles to get there and additionally had no grant at that time to spend on tapes and secretaries, so that I had to type out my notes between visits.

I discovered the extent of my own involvement with surprise on several occasions. After spending a month or so on the Project, I discovered in passing a bathroom mirror at the school that I looked pale and realized that I had expected to see a black face. After spending two months at Hawthorne House, I spent some moments on a subway looking idly at a fat man's stomach before I realized he couldn't be pregnant. While these are trivial examples, it seemed to me both in gathering data and in writing about girls' experiences, I relied a great deal on my own self-involvement. For while my field notes are a record of what I saw and heard, they also serve to recall the sense of what happened from within myself. I found this to be a check against a kind of easy sociological cynicism, on the one hand, and an overly sentimental concern for the plights of various girls, on the other.

While my participation in the two institutions put me in touch with some of the external circumstances and some of the internal sense of girls' experiences there, I found some limitations in my data, particularly as I began to compare the Project with Hawthorne House.

Because Hawthorne House was a more total institution, a greater variety of situations were organized by the institution and were more easily accessible. The primary situations in which I was routinely *not* involved were private interviews between the social workers and girls and labor in the hospital; and while I visited girls in the hospital, I only visited girls I knew well.

On the Project, for a variety of good and bad reasons, I was routinely *not* involved in a greater number of situations. While I did go home after school with several girls who became out-of-school friends of each other and of mine, I usually felt this to be a difficult situation in relation to their families. Participant-observation requires a kind of equality and a special kind of permission. In going to girls' homes I was really going to their parents' homes, and I could not convince myself the Project permission, or the girls' permission gave me the right to intrude in family life.

While the Project, primarily a school, involved fewer aspects of their clients' lives than Hawthorne House, this was particularly true around the time of delivery. The Project required girls to stay home several weeks before they were due to deliver and to remain at home some weeks following delivery. Because my original concerns were with the effects of institutions, I tended generally to confine myself to the limits of the institution.

For reasons of reluctance and the boundaries of the Project, therefore, I did not cover the weeks immediately before and after delivery, although I shared girls' accounts upon their return to school. I now regard this as a mistake, for it made for a lacuna in comparing the experiences of the Project and Hawthorne House girls. In my own research, it was a mistake which points again to the particular time pressures inherent in participant-observation. My activities on the Project, in contrast to Hawthorne House, were not funded which meant my time was continuously limited by the necessity to accumulate notes by hand. Participant-observation, particularly among unwed mothers, cannot be intermittently spread over time without losing the context in which events make sense, and in my case, without losing the persons I knew. Less crowded by time, I believe I would not have made the mistake described.

Finally, one of the special features of participant-observation, particularly for comparative purposes, concerns what is *not* said. For example, I noticed during my stay at Hawthorne House, after my stay on the Project, that the girls at Hawthorne House spoke a great deal about becoming a mother, while the Project girls had not. This difference could be interpreted in a variety of ways. It could be viewed as meaningless—that the Project girls, in speaking instead of "having a baby" simply chose different terms for the same concern. Or the Project girls might have expressed a concern for becoming a mother in response to a direct question. I chose to understand the difference as meaningfully related to the circumstances of the two groups of girls.

Because field data are gathered as much by listening as by questioning (this being its special advantage over methods of formal questioning), concern with what may *not* be being said creates a kind of tension in the observer who wishes to allow events to develop spontaneously on the one hand, while he wishes the events to bear on certain issues on the other hand. It is a tension reflected in field data, either in gaps of information or gaps in natural history.

The Contraceptive History Interviews

Data regarding knowledge, use, and feelings about contraceptive methods were collected from about half the female students at a small, co-ed college with an interview schedule administered by five girls who were themselves students at the same college. The schedule was predetermined and fixed but included a number of possibilities for probing by the interviewer.

The interviewers were picked on the basis of previous interviewing experience and general competence and were trained for this task in the process of using the schedule on each other. I chose female interviewers because evidence as well as common sense suggests that they would obtain this sort of data more easily than males (Benney, Riesman, and Star, 1956). Because the interview was a personal one, although no enquiry was made about other than the contraceptive aspects of the girls' sexual lives, and because of my own position at the college, I did not wish to do the interviewing myself. I should also observe that in a larger college, and in a college where students are less openly committed to the acceptability of sexual relations, I would not have used peer interviewers but would have done the interviewing myself.

Because I also did not wish to know who was interviewed, I left the selection of interviewees to my interviewers who organized the matter of selection so that the same girl would not be approached twice. The interviewers, who usually approached acquaintances first, themselves represented each class in the college, as well as different social groups within the college.

While randomness was not relevant to the uses I wished to make of the data and while bias is difficult to assess, any bias is probably toward inclusion of a greater proportion of sexually experienced girls. Only one interviewer was sexually inexperienced, and she tended to interview girls who were also inexperienced. However, she was a first-year student and selected first-year students who are less experienced and were not underrepresented in the total number of interviews.

The one bias which would affect the uses I have made of

these data would be an underrepresentation of "free spirits" —girls for whom neither sexual relations nor contraception have ever been at moral issue. The number of girls interviewed who had come to a position of this sort, but who had done so by overcoming past ambivalences and guilts, suggests that this bias probably did not exist. Furthermore, as I have said, the college population was itself biased toward sexual experience in relation to other college populations. This was in fact my reason for interviewing there.

For reasons of the college atmosphere, it is likely that any biasing of responses given in the actual interview would be toward *rationality* about sexual relations and contraception; as I have said, change in the direction of *rationality* about contraception was one unintended effect of the interview. This potential bias is not a problem, however, for it works against my interpretation rather than falsely for it. Furthermore, it is likely that girls who report past or current ambivalence over the issue of contraception are more like girls elsewhere.

Each of the decisions I have described—the use of female peers as interviewers, interviewer selection of interviewees, the withholding of names from me and my nonparticipation, and the focus on contraception but not on sexual histories— were made to maximize ease and minimize refusal and were made in relation to the character of the college. One refusal was reported.

The interviewers were also given some degree of freedom to pursue additional questions if the tone of the interview warranted it. For example, they could ask, as they frequently did if the context seemed to warrant it, if the interviewee had ever suspected she was pregnant, what she did, etc. If girls volunteered they had been pregnant and were willing to talk about what they had done, the interviewer pursued the topic.

This approach netted one very interesting interview with

a girl who solved the problem of illegitimate pregnancy by getting married and spoke of going back home with her baby in much the same terms as the Project girls:

> I knew that being from a small town, people were going to talk. Like even if the baby was born two years later people would still talk. But in my hometown, of all the girls getting married, only one of them wasn't pregnant. So I knew I wouldn't feel too uncomfortable about it. It wasn't like I was the only one. Still, I feel a little uncomfortable going back there now (being obviously pregnant), but I know that after the baby's born I'm going to take the baby there and I'll be proud. I won't care what anyone says.

While the methodology of this as well as other aspects of the study may appear excessively eclectic or loose, it has allowed participants and researchers to talk to each other in ways that have been, to some extent, constrained and reflected on in terms of scientific objectivity, but not so much so that girls' thoughts and views of the world were hidden by mechanical notions of scientific procedure.

Bibliography

Adams, H. M., and U. M. Gallagher. "Some Facts and Observations about Illegitimacy," *Children*, 10 (1963): 43–48.

Anschuetz, M. "Five College Girls' Decisions to Use Birth Control Pills," unpublished manuscript, 23 pp., 1967.

De Beauvoir, Simone. *The Second Sex*. New York: Alfred A. Knopf, 1952.

Bell, Robert R. *Premarital Sex in a Changing Society*. Englewood Cliffs, N.J.: Prentice-Hall, 1966.

Benney, M., D. Riesman, and S. A. Star. "Age and Sex in the Interview," *American Journal of Sociology*, 62 (1956): 143–152.

Bernstein, R. "Gaps in Services to Unmarried Mothers," *Children*, 10 (1963): 49–54.

Bowerman, Charles E., Donald P. Irish, and Hallowell Pope. *Unwed Motherhood: Personal and Social Consequences*. Chapel Hill: University of North Carolina Institute for Research in Social Science, 1963–1966, 419 pp.

Coombs, L. C., R. Freedman, J. Friedman, and W. F. Pratt. "Premarital Pregnancy and Status Before and After Marriage," *American Journal of Sociology*, 75 (1970): 800–820.

Ehrmann, Winston. *Premarital Dating Behavior*. New York: Bantam Books, 1960.

Furstenberg, F., L. Gordis, and M. Markowitz. "Birth Control Knowledge and Attitudes among Unmarried Pregnant Adolescents: A Preliminary Report," *Journal of Marriage and the Family*, 31 (1969): 34–47.

Garfinkel, Harold. *Studies in Ethnomethodology*. Englewood Cliffs, N.J.: Prentice-Hall, 1967.

Gebhard, Paul H., Wardell B. Pomeroy, Clyde E. Martin, and Cornelia Christenson. *Pregnancy, Birth and Abortion*. New York: John Wiley, 1958.

Goffman, Erving. *The Presentation of Self in Everyday Life*. Chicago: Aldine, 1959.

_____. *Asylums*. Garden City, N.Y.: Doubleday, 1961.

_____. *Stigma*. Englewood Cliffs, N.J.: Prentice-Hall Spectrum Books, 1963.

Hammond, B. E. "The Contest System: A Survival Technique." Master's thesis, Washington University, St. Louis, Missouri, 44 pp., 1965.

Hammond, B. E., and J. Ladner. "Socialization into Sexual Behavior in a Negro Slum Ghetto," in Carlford B. Broderick and Jessie Bernard (eds.), *The Individual, Sex, and Society* (Baltimore, Md.: The Johns Hopkins Press, 1969): pp. 41–51.

Jones, Wyatt. "Review of the Literature Relating to Unmarried Mothers," unpublished manuscript, 10 pp., 1967.

Kinsey, Alfred C., Wardell B. Pomeroy, Clyde E. Martin, and Paul H. Gebhard. *Sexual Behavior in the Human Female*. New York: Simon & Schuster, 1953.

Ladner, J. A. "Deviance in the Lower Class Adolescent Sub-Culture." Master's thesis, Washington University, St. Louis, Missouri, 51 pp., 1966.

Lee, Nancy Howell. *The Search for an Abortionist*. Chicago: The University of Chicago Press, 1969.

Liebow, Elliot. "Fathers without Children," *Public Interest*, 5 (Fall, 1966): 13–25.

_____. *Tally's Corner*. Boston: Little, Brown, 1967.

Matza, David. *Delinquency and Drift*. New York: John Wiley, 1964.

Perlman, H. H. "Unmarried Mothers," in Nathan E. Cohen (ed.), *Social Work and Social Problems* (New York: National Association of Social Workers, 1964).

Rainwater, Lee. *And the Poor Get Children.* Chicago: Quadrangle Books, 1960.

_____. *Family Design.* Chicago: Aldine, 1965.

_____. "The Problem of Lower Class Culture," unpublished manuscript prepared for Sociology Department Colloquium, University of Wisconsin, September 23, 1966.

_____. "Sex in the Culture of Poverty," in Carlford B. Broderick and Jessie Bernard (eds.), *The Individual, Sex, and Society* (Baltimore, Md.: The Johns Hopkins Press, 1969): pp. 129–140.

_____. *Behind Ghetto Walls.* Chicago: Aldine, 1970.

Reiss, A. J. "The Social Integration of Queers and Peers," *Social Problems,* 9 (1961): 102–120.

Reiss, Ira L. *Premarital Sexual Standards in America.* New York: Free Press, 1960.

_____. *The Social Context of Premarital Sexual Permissiveness.* New York: Holt, Rinehart and Winston, 1967.

Riesman, David. "The Sociology of the Interview," in David Riesman, *Abundance For What?* (Garden City, N.Y.: Doubleday Anchor, 1964): pp. 492–513.

Roth, Julius A. *Timetables.* Indianapolis: Bobbs-Merrill, 1963.

Schofield, Michael. *The Sexual Behavior of Young People.* Boston: Little, Brown, 1965.

Short, J. F., F. Strodtbeck, and D. Cartwright. "A Strategy for Utilizing Research Dilemmas: A Case from the Study of Parenthood in a Street Corner Gang," *Sociological Inquiry,* 32 (1962): 185–202.

Short, James F., and Fred L. Strodtbeck. *Group Process and Gang Delinquency.* Chicago: University of Chicago Press, 1965.

Strodtbeck, F., and J. Short. "Aleatory Risks vs. Short-Run Hedonism in Explanations of Gang Action," *Social Problems,* 12 (1964): 127–140.

Sudnow, David. *Passing On.* Englewood Cliffs, N.J.: Prentice-Hall, 1967.

Sykes, G. M., and D. Matza. "Techniques of Neutralization: A Theory of Delinquency," *American Sociological Review,* 22 (1957): 664–670.

Teele, J. E., D. Robinson, W. Schmidt, and E. P. Rice. "Factors Related to Social Work Services for Mothers of Babies Born Out of Wedlock," paper presented at the 94th Annual Meeting, American Public Health Association, San Francisco, November, 1966.

Thompson, Jean. *The House of Tomorrow*. New York: Harper & Row, 1967.

Vincent, Clark E. *Unmarried Mothers*. New York: Free Press, 1961.

Willy, L. R. "The Social Context of Unwed Motherhood," Unpublished Master's thesis, University of Texas, August, 1965.

Index

203